The [Best of] ... Attic

A YEAR OF
AFGHANS ™

52 project ... **of the year**

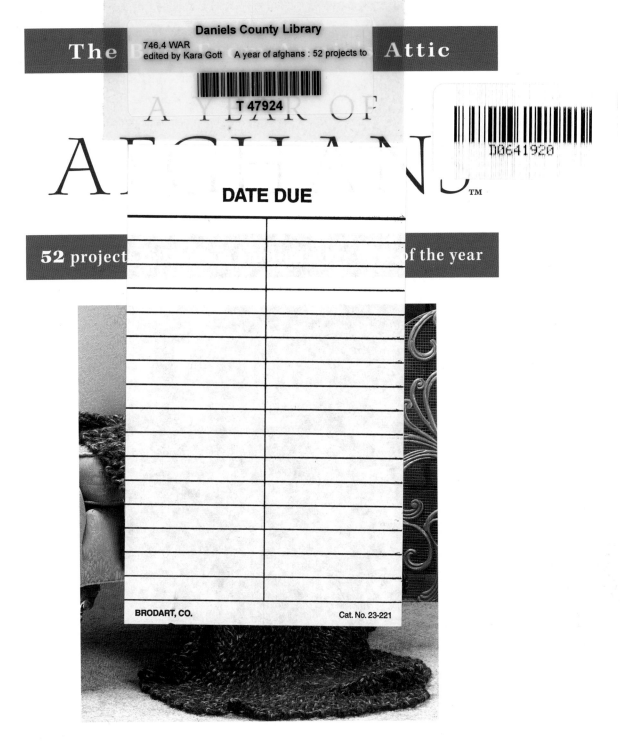

Edited by Kara Gott Warner

HOUSE of
WHITE
BIRCHES

PUBLISHERS
SINCE 1947

A YEAR OF AFGHANS™

EDITOR Kara Gott Warner
ART DIRECTOR Brad Snow
PUBLISHING SERVICES DIRECTOR Brenda Gallmeyer

EDITORIAL ASSISTANTS Jill Case, Laurie Lehman
ASSISTANT ART DIRECTOR Nick Pierce
COPY SUPERVISOR Deborah Morgan
COPY EDITORS Emily Carter, Mary O'Donnell
TECHNICAL EDITOR Kathy Wesley
TECHNICAL ARTIST Debbie Kuntz

PRODUCTION ARTIST SUPERVISOR Erin Augsburger
GRAPHIC ARTISTS Debby Keel, Amanda Treharn
PRODUCTION ASSISTANTS Marj Morgan, Judy Neuenschwander

PHOTOGRAPHY SUPERVISOR Tammy Christian
PHOTOGRAPHY Matthew Owen
PHOTO STYLISTS Tammy Liechty, Tammy Steiner

Printed in the United States of America
Library of Congress Number: 2011900836
Softcover ISBN: 978-1-59217-336-5

A Year of Afghans is published by DRG, 306 East Parr Road, Berne, IN 46711.

1 2 3 4 5 6 7 8 9

Introduction

. . . .

When we think of knitted afghans, the adjectives that often come to mind are: cozy, comforting, cuddly and warm. There's something special about making one of these timeless creations, because they never go out of style. Beyond the practical reasons for surrounding ourselves with our favorite throws, they also hold sentimental value. For example, they often evoke fond memories and thoughts of loved ones; or, they may have been handed down through several generations. Whatever your reasons for holding on to your treasured afghans, you'll find an exciting group of designs to add to your favored collection on the pages that follow.

A Year of Afghans features a variety of designs from the simplest stitch combinations to skill-building projects that incorporate cables, textured stitches, slipped stitches, bobble accents, mitering and color work. Are you looking for the sweetest blankie for baby, or something to give to your favorite charity? Maybe you're looking to simply enhance your home decor. Whatever your reasons for embarking on your next afghan, I'm sure you'll be satisfied by the compilation of projects we've assembled.

As you browse through the pages within, you'll find page after page of eye-popping designs to keep you in stitches all year long!

Kara

Kara Gott Warner, editor

Leafy Splendor,
page 17

Clear Skies,
page 30

Sedona Reds Throw,
page 57

Table of Contents

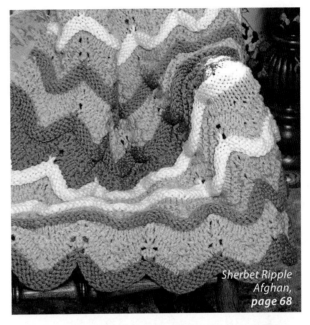

Sherbet Ripple Afghan, page 68

Sweet Hearts Baby Blanket, page 97

Block Party

This interesting assortment of afghans will introduce you to methods for working easy blocks, and if you're interested in learning a new technique, you'll be amazed at how much fun making mitered blocks can be!

Positive/Negative Afghan

Colors change position in a cozy, geometrically inspired afghan.

Design by Svetlana Avrakh

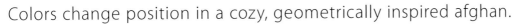

Skill Level

■■■□ INTERMEDIATE

Finished Size
Approx 55 x 67 inches

Materials
- Patons Decor (worsted weight; 75% acrylic/25% wool; 208 yds/100g per skein): 9 skeins taupe #87631 (A), 7 skeins aran #87602 (B)
- Size 4 (3.5mm) 36-inch circular needle or size needed to obtain gauge

4 MEDIUM

Gauge
21 sts and 25 rows = 4 inches/10cm in color pat.

To save time, take time to check gauge.

Special Abbreviation
Increase (inc): Inc 1 by knitting or purling in front and then back of st.

Pattern Note
Circular needle is used to accommodate large number of stitches; do not join, work back and forth in rows.

Panel A
Make 3

With B, cast on 47 sts.

*Referring to Color Block chart, work Rows 1–56 in St st, using B as background color and A for contrast.

Rep Rows 1–56 of Color Block chart, using A as background color and B for contrast.

Rep from * twice—6 Color Blocks in all.

Bind off.

Panel B
Make 2

With A, cast on 47 sts.

Work as for Panel A, reversing color positions.

Sew panels tog in following sequence: A, B, A, B, A.

Color Blocks should alternate positions and form a checkerboard pat.

Top & Bottom Borders
With RS facing and A, pick up and knit 217 sts along bound-off edge of afghan.

Purl 3 rows, inc 1 st each end on 2nd row and inc 15 sts evenly across last row—234 sts.

Work in pat from Border chart, continue with A as background color and B as contrast, inc 1 st each end on 3rd row, then every RS row.

With background color, knit 4 rows, inc 1 st each end every other row as before.

Bind off kwise on WS.

Rep for bottom border by picking up sts along cast-on edge.

Side Borders
With RS facing and background color, pick up and knit 256 sts along 1 side edge.

Purl 3 rows, inc 1 st each end on 2nd row and inc 26 sts evenly across last row—284 sts.

Work as for top/bottom borders.

Rep for 2nd side.

Sew corner edges tog.

Block. ●

COLOR KEY
☐ Background
● Contrast

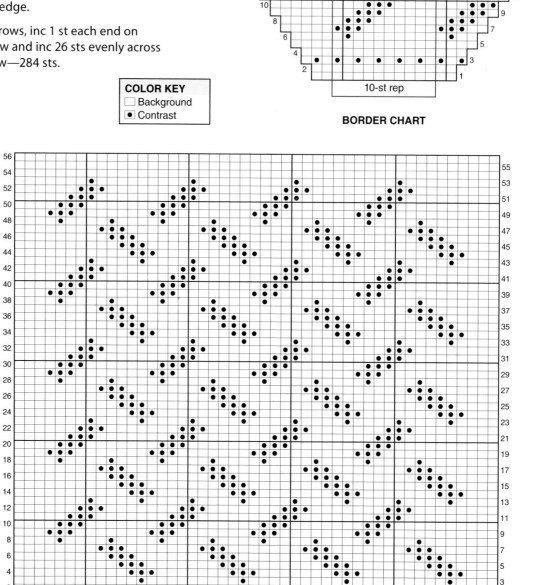

BORDER CHART

COLOR BLOCK CHART

Make It Mitered Afghan

They'll think you spent hours changing colors … only you will know this wonderful yarn did a lot of the work.

Design by JoAnne Turcotte for Plymouth Yarn Co.

. . . .

Skill Level
■■□□ EASY

Finished Size
Approx 45 x 55 inches

Materials
- Plymouth Yarn Co. Boku (worsted weight; 95% wool/5% silk; 99 yds/50g per ball): 24 balls variegated #12
- Size 8 (5mm) needles or size needed to obtain gauge
- Size 9 (5.5mm) needles
- Size G/6 (4mm) crochet hook (optional)
- Stitch marker

Gauge
14 sts = 4 inches/10cm in pat with smaller needles.

To save time, take time to check gauge.

Special Abbreviation
Central Double Decrease (CDD): Sl next 2 sts as if to k2tog, k1, p2sso.

Pattern Note
The figures show squares in 2 colors for ease of description. Only 1 yarn is used in the afghan. Also, Figure 4 shows only 9 rows; there are a total of 21 rows of squares in the afghan.

Basic Mitered Square
With larger needle, very loosely cast on 29 sts. Change to smaller needles.

Row 1 (WS): Knit.

Row 2 (RS): K13, CDD, k13.

Row 3: Purl.

Row 4: K12, CDD, k12.

Row 5: Knit to center st (k12), purl center st, knit to end of row—k12.

Row 6: K11, CDD, k11.

Row 7: Purl.

Row 8: K10, CDD, k10.

Row 9: K10, purl center st, k10.

Row 10: K9, CDD, k9.

Row 11: Purl.

Row 12: K8, CDD, k8.

Row 13: K8, purl center st, k8.

Row 14: K7, CDD, k7.

Row 15: Purl.

Row 16: K6, CDD, k6.

Row 17: K6, purl center st, k6.

Row 18: K5, CDD, k5.

Row 19: Purl.

Row 20: K4, CDD, k4.

Row 21: K4, purl center st, k4.

Row 22: K3, CDD, k3.

Row 23: Purl.

Row 24: K2, CDD, k2.

Row 25: K2, purl center st, k2.

Row 26: K1, CDD, k1.

Row 27: Purl.

Row 28: Work CDD. Pull yarn through rem st; fasten off.

Rep Rows 1–28 for each square.

Afghan

First Row
Work 9 basic mitered squares; when 9 squares are completed, lay 2 squares side by side (Figure 1). These first-row squares are shown in blue.

Second Row
Beg at RH edge with RS facing, work next row of 8 squares (shown in red). Referring to Figure 1 and Figure 2, pick up and knit 14 sts on downward sloping right edge of square #1, 1 st at lower point, and 14 sts along upward sloping left edge of square #2. Work Rows 1–28 of Basic Mitered Square (Figure 3).

Continue to work in this manner until 8 squares are completed for 2nd row.

Third Row
For Row 3 (shown in blue), make RH side square:

Cast on 14 sts, pick up and knit 1 st in corner and 14 sts along left sloping edge of first red square.

Complete by working Rows 1–28, then work next 7 squares as above.

Work LH edge square of row; pick up and knit 14 sts along downward sloping right edge of last red square, 1 st in corner, then cast on 14 sts—29 sts.

Work Rows 1–28 of Basic Mitered Square.

Rem Rows
Rep 2nd and 3rd rows for a total of 21 rows—179 squares.

Fasten off.

Border (Optional)
With crochet hook, work a border of sc around afghan if desired. ●

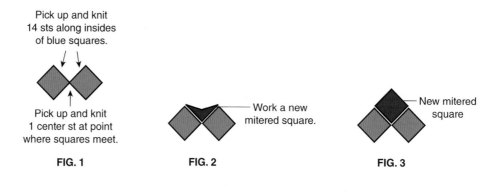

Pick up and knit 14 sts along insides of blue squares.

Pick up and knit 1 center st at point where squares meet.

FIG. 1

Work a new mitered square.

FIG. 2

New mitered square

FIG. 3

FIG. 4

Kaleidoscope Throw

It's so easy, even a beginner can tackle this throw with beautiful results!
Just knit the strips, sew them together and add tassels.

Design by George Shaheen

· ·

Skill Level

■□□□ BEGINNER

Finished Size
Approx 45 inches square (excluding tassels)

Materials
- Lion Brand Yarn Wool-Ease Chunky (bulky weight; 80% acrylic/20% wool; 153 yds/140g per ball): 3 balls willow #173 (A); 2 balls evergreen #180 (E); 1 ball each of orchid #146 (B), deep rose #140 (C) and pumpkin #133 (D)
- Size 11 (8mm) knitting needles or size needed to obtain gauge
- Tapestry needle
- 6-inch piece of cardboard

Gauge
11 sts and 20 rows = 4 inches in garter st (knit every row).

To save time, take time to check gauge.

Strip A
Make 2

With A, cast on 14 sts.

Rows 1–24: Knit.

Bind off.

Strip B
Make 2

With A, cast on 14 sts.

Rows 1–24: Knit. At end of Row 24, cut A.

Rows 25–48: With B, knit. At end of Row 48, cut B.

Rows 49–72: With A, knit.

Bind off.

Strip C
Make 2

With A, cast on 14 sts.

Rows 1–24: Knit. At end of Row 24, cut A.

Rows 25–48: With D, knit. At end of Row 48, cut D.

Rows 49–72: With A, knit. At end of Row 72, cut A.

Rows 73–96: With D, knit. At end of Row 96, cut D.

Rows 97–120: With A, knit.

Bind off.

Strip D
Make 2

With A, cast on 14 sts.

Rows 1–24: Knit. At end of Row 24, cut A.

Rows 25–48: With C, knit. At end of Row 48, cut C.

Rows 49–72: With A, knit. At end of Row 72, cut A.

Rows 73–96: With C, knit. At end of Row 96, cut C.

Rows 97–120: With A, knit. At end of Row 120, cut A.

Rows 121–144: With C, knit. At end of Row 144, cut C.

Row 145–168: With A, knit.

Bind off.

Strip E
Make 1

With A, cast on 14 sts.

Rows 1–24: Knit. At end of Row 24, cut A.

Rows 25–48: With B, knit. At end of Row 48, cut B.

Rows 49–72: With A, knit. At end of Row 72, cut A.

Rows 73–96: With B, knit. At end of Row 96, cut B.

Rows 97–120: With A, knit. At end of Row 120, cut A.

Rows 121–144: With B, knit. At end of Row 144, cut B.

Rows 145–168: With A, knit. At end of Row 168, cut A.

Rows 169–192: With B, knit. At end of Row 192, cut B.

Rows 193–216: With A, knit.

Bind off.

Finishing
Referring to Assembly Diagram for placement, with A, sew strips tog.

Tassel
Make 20

Cut 1 (12-inch) length of E and place it across top of 6-inch length of cardboard. Wrap E 18 times around cardboard over strand at top. Tie 12-inch length tightly at top of tassel, leaving ends for finishing. Cut ends at bottom and remove from cardboard. Cut 16-inch length of E and tie it twice around tassel about 1 inch from top. With lengths left for finishing, tie tassel at 1 outer edge point. Trim ends even. ●

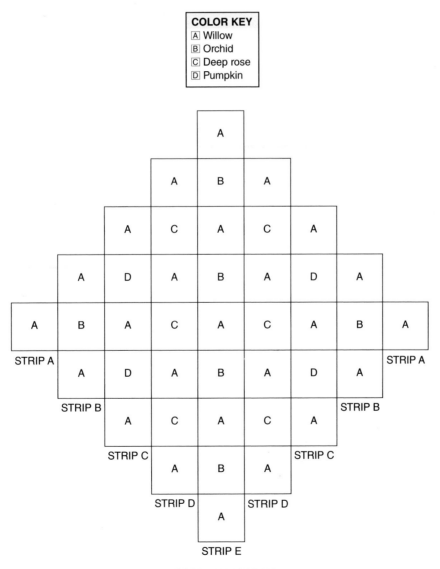

ASSEMBLY DIAGRAM

Leafy Splendor

Autumn's colorful palette is the inspiration for an afghan to love.

Design by Debby Ware

. . . .

Skill Level
■■□□ EASY

Finished Size
Approx 48 x 48 inches

Materials
- Cascade Yarns 220 Superwash (worsted weight; 100% superwash wool; 220 yds/100g per skein): 2 skeins each lime green #887, pumpkin #825, light brown #853, dark brown #858, burgundy #893, greenish gray #1919, gray #1926, olive #891, pale cream #878
- 3 size 7 (4.5mm) needles and 2 double-point needles or size needed to obtain gauge

Gauge
18 sts = 4 inches/10cm in garter st.

Exact gauge is not critical to this project.

Special Abbreviations
Make 1 (M1): Inc by making a backward loop over right needle.

Central Double Decrease (CDD): Slip next 2 sts as if to k2tog, k1, p2sso.

Special Technique
3-Needle Bind-Off: Hold blocks with RS tog and tips of 2 needles facing in same direction. Using a 3rd needle, *insert RH needle into first st on front needle and then first st on back needle and knit these 2 sts tog; rep from * once more and pass first st on RH needle over 2nd st on RH needle. Continue in same manner until all sts are worked tog. Pull yarn through last st.

Block
Make 25 in assorted colors

Cast on 38 sts and knit 3 rows.

Row 1: Knit across.

Row 2: K3, purl to last 3 sts, k3.

Row 3: K3, [p2, k1] 10 times, end p2, k3.

Row 4: K3, [k2, p1] 10 times, end k5.

[Rep Rows 1–4] 10 times.

Knit 3 rows. Bind off all sts.

Assembly
Place blocks, as desired, in 5 rows of 5 blocks each. With desired color (sample uses lime green) and RS facing, pick up and knit 26 sts in ends of rows along side of first block. Knit 4 rows (2 ridges garter st).

With 2nd needle, pick up and knit 26 sts in ends of rows along edge of next block. Knit 4 rows. With RS of blocks facing, bind off edges tog, using 3-needle bind-off.

Continue to join blocks into 5 rows of 5 blocks each.

To join strips, pick up and knit 1 st in each st along edge of strip, having same number of sts in each block. Pick up and knit same number of sts on edge of next strip and bind off all sts tog, being careful to align blocks.

Large Leaf
Make 24 in assorted colors

Cast on 10 sts.

Row 1: K10, cast on 9 sts—19 sts.

Row 2: K1, M1, k7, CDD, k7, M1, k1—19 sts.

Row 3: P19.

Row 4: P9, k1, p9.

Row 5: K9, p1, k9.

Rows 6–17: [Rep Rows 2–5] 3 times.

Row 18: K8, CDD, k8—17 sts.

Row 19: P17.

Row 33: K4, p3tog, k4—9 sts.

Row 34: K3, CDD, k3—7 sts.

Row 35: P7.

Row 36: P3, k1, p3.

Row 37: K2, p3tog, k2—5 sts.

Row 38: K1, CDD, k1—3 sts.

Row 39: P3.

Row 40: K3tog. Fasten off.

Small Leaf

Make 12 in assorted colors (3 for each corner)

Cast on 15 sts.

Row 1: K6, CDD, k6—13 sts.

Row 2: K6, p1, k6.

Row 3: K5, CDD, k5—11 sts.

Row 4: K5, p1, k5.

Row 5: K4, CDD, k4—9 sts.

Row 6: K4, p1, k4.

Row 7: K3, CDD, k3—7 sts.

Row 8: K3, p1, k3.

Row 9: K2, CDD, k2—5 sts.

Row 10: K2, p1, k2.

Row 11: K1, CDD, k1—3 sts.

Place rem 3 sts on dpn, *sl sts to other end of needle, pull yarn across back, k3, rep from * for about 5 rows. K3tog and fasten off, leaving a 3-inch tail.

Referring to photo, place large leaves on blocks in a pleasing arrangement, leaving center block empty. Sew each leaf in place using running st and color of block.

Attach 3 small leaves to each corner, using 3-inch tails. ●

Row 20: P8, k1, p8.

Row 21: K8, p1, k8.

Row 22: K7, CDD, k7—15 sts.

Row 23: P15.

Row 24: P7, k1, p7.

Row 25: K7, p1, k7.

Row 26: K6, CDD, k6—13 sts.

Row 27: P13.

Row 28: P6, k1, p6.

Row 29: K6, p1, k6.

Row 30: K5, CDD, k5—11 sts.

Row 31: P11.

Row 32: P5, k1, p5.

Mitered Squares & Stripes Throw

Use four shades of yarn for this fresh and easy approach to a mitered-square throw.

Design by Lisa Carnahan for N.Y. Yarns

. . . .

Skill Level

■■■□ INTERMEDIATE

Finished Size
Approx 44 x 60 inches

Materials
- N.Y. Yarns Olympic (worsted weight; 70% acrylic/30% wool; 130 yds/ 50g per ball): 5 balls each cream #1 (A), cactus #5 (B), sapphire #7 (C), 3 balls cornflower #6 (D)
- Size 10 (6mm) 16- and 24-inch circular needles or size needed to obtain gauge
- Stitch markers

4 MEDIUM

Gauge
14 sts = 4 inches/10cm in garter st.

To save time, take time to check gauge.

Stripe Panel Sequence
With B, knit 3 rows.

With A, knit 2 rows.

With C, knit 4 rows.

With D, knit 4 rows.

With C, knit 4 rows.

With A, knit 2 rows.

With B, knit 4 rows.

Basic Mitered Square
Note: Set-up row counts as Row 1 of pat; beg square with Row 2.

Work 6 rows each of A, B, C, D, A, B, C, D.

Row 1 (RS): Knit across.

Row 2: Knit to 2 sts before marker, ssk, sl marker, k2tog, knit to end.

Rep Rows 1 and 2 for pat.

After completion of color sequence, 2 sts rem. Bind off 2 sts.

Throw
With B, and longer circular needle, cast on 125 sts.

Work Stripe Panel Sequence.

Right Mitered Squares
Set-up row for first mitered square: With A and shorter circular needle, cast on 25 sts, place marker; knit across first 25 sts of longer needle. Leave rem sts on longer needle.

Beg with Row 2, work Basic Mitered Square.

Setup row for 2nd, 3rd, 4th and 5th mitered squares: With A and shorter needle, pick up 25 sts along left edge of previous square, place marker; knit across next 25 sts of longer needle. Beg with Row 2, work Basic Mitered Square.

Stripe Panel
With B and longer needle, pick up and knit 125 sts along top edges of squares. Work Stripe Panel Sequence.

Left Mitered Squares
Set-up row for first mitered square: Place 25 sts from left side of longer needle onto shorter needle, leave rem sts on longer needle.

With A, knit across these 25 sts, place marker; cast on 25 sts. Beg with Row 2, work Basic Mitered Square.

Set-up row for 2nd, 3rd, 4th and 5th mitered squares: Sl next 25 sts from left side of longer needle onto shorter needle. With A, knit across these 25 sts, place marker; pick up and knit 25 sts along right edge of previous square. Beg with Row 2, work Basic Mitered Square.

With B, pick up and knit 125 sts along top edges of squares. Work Stripe Panel Sequence.

Rep from from Right Mitered Squares once more, then work Right Mitered Squares and Stripe Panel Sequence once more (6 stripes and 5 rows of squares). With B, bind off all sts.

Side Stripe Panel
With B and longer needle, pick up and knit 197 sts along side edge.

Work stripe panel. With B, bind off all sts.

Rep stripe panel on other side edge. ●

Easy Does It

If you're in need of some instant gratification, this chapter will satisfy.
We've got quick and easy throws and afghans that you can make in a
flash. Projects made in chunky-weight yarn, or with several strands held
together, make these creations toasty warm!

Sumptuous Slants

Chunky chenille stripes add a soft touch to this richly textured afghan, worked diagonally from corner to corner.

Design by George Shaheen

Skill Level
■■■□ INTERMEDIATE

Finished Size
52 x 75 inches

Materials
- Red Heart Super Saver (worsted weight; 100% acrylic; 364 yds/198g per skein): 9 skeins medium purple #528 (A)
- Lion Brand Quick & Cozy (super bulky weight; 100% nylon; 55 yds/100g per skein): 2 skeins each blueberry #110 (B), olive #174 (C) and chocolate #126 (D)
- Size 17 (12.75mm) circular knitting needle or size needed to obtain gauge
- Size 15 (10mm) circular knitting needle
- Tapestry needle

Gauge
19 sts = 10 inches/25cm in garter st (knit every row) with larger needle and 3 strands of worsted weight yarn held tog.

To save time, take time to check gauge.

Special Abbreviation
Increase (inc): Knit into front and back of next st.

Pattern Notes
Main pattern is worked with 3 strands of A held together, and stripes are worked with 1 strand of B, C or D.

Afghan is worked diagonally from lower left corner to upper right corner.

Circular needles are used to accommodate large number of stitches; do not join, work back and forth in rows.

Due to nature of pattern, finished afghan will not be a perfect rectangle and will need to be blocked to given measurements.

Afghan
With larger needle and A, cast on 3 sts.

Row 1 (RS): K1, yo, k2—4 sts.

Row 2: K1, yo, k2tog, yo, k1—5 sts.

Row 3: K2, yo, k2tog, yo, k1—6 sts.

Row 4: K2, yo, k2tog, yo, k2—7 sts.

Row 5: K1, *yo, k2tog; rep from * to last 2 sts, yo, k2—8 sts.

Row 6: K1, *yo, k2tog; rep from * to last st, yo, k1—9 sts.

Row 7: K2, *yo, k2tog; rep from * to last st, yo, k1—10 sts.

Row 8: K2, *yo, k2tog; rep from * to last 2 sts, yo, k2—11 sts.

Rows 9–28: [Rep Rows 5–8] 5 times—31 sts.

Cut A, join B.

Change to smaller needle.

Rows 29 and 30: Knit to last st, inc—33 sts.

Cut B, join C.

Rows 31–34: Rep Row 29—37 sts.

Cut C, join B.

Rows 35 and 36: Rep Row 29—39 sts.

Cut B, join A.

Row 37: Rep Row 29—40 sts.

Change to larger needle.

Rows 38–40: Rep Rows 6–8—43 sts.

Rows 41–68: [Rep Rows 5–8] 7 times—71 sts.

Cut A, join B.

Change to smaller needle.

Rows 69 and 70: Rep Row 29—73 sts.

Cut B, join D.

Rows 71–74: Rep Row 29—77 sts.

Cut D, join B.

Rows 75 and 76: Rep Row 29—79 sts.

Cut B, join A.

Row 77: Rep Row 29—80 sts.

Change to larger needle.

Rows 78–80: Rep Rows 6–8—83 sts.

Rows 81–108: [Rep Rows 5–8] 7 times—111 sts.

Cut A, join B.

Change to smaller needle.

Rows 109 and 110: Rep Row 29—113 sts.

Cut B, join C.

Rows 111–114: Rep Row 29—117 sts.

Cut C, join B.

Row 115: Rep Row 29—118 sts.

Row 116: Knit to last 2 sts, k2tog—117 sts.

Cut B, join A.

Row 117: Rep Row 29—118 sts.

Change to larger needle.

Row 118: K1, *yo, k2tog; rep from * to last st, k1.

Row 119: K1, *k2tog, yo; rep from * to last st, k1.

Row 120: K2, *yo, k2tog; rep from * to last 2 sts, k2.

Row 121: K2, *k2tog, yo; rep from * to last 2 sts, k2.

Rows 122–145: [Rep Rows 118–121] 6 times.

Rows 146–148: Rep Rows 118–120.

Cut A, join B.

Change to smaller needle.

Row 149: Knit.

Row 150: Rep Row 116—117 sts.

Cut B, join D.

Rows 151–154: Rep Row 116—113 sts.

Cut D, join B.

Rows 155 and 156: Rep Row 116—111 sts.

Cut B, join A.

Row 157: Rep Row 116—110 sts.

Change to larger needle.

Row 158: K2, *k2tog, yo; rep from * to last 4 sts, k2tog, k2—109 sts.

Row 159: K2, *k2tog, yo; rep from * to last 3 sts, k2tog, k1—108 sts.

Row 160: K1, *k2tog, yo; rep from * to last 3 sts, k2tog, k1—107 sts.

Row 161: K1, *k2tog, yo; rep from * to last 4 sts, k2tog, k2—106 sts.

Rows 162–185: [Rep Rows 158–161] 6 times—82 sts.

Rows 186–188: Rep Rows 158–160—79 sts.

Cut A, join B.

Change to smaller needle.

Rows 189 and 190: Rep Row 116—77 sts.

Cut B, join C.

Rows 191–194: Rep Row 116—73 sts.

Cut C, join B.

Rows 195 and 196: Rep Row 116—71 sts.

Cut B, join A.

Row 197: Rep Row 116—70 sts.

Change to larger needle.

Rows 198–225: [Rep Rows 158–161] 7 times—42 sts.

Rows 226–228: Rep Rows 158–160—39 sts.

Cut A, join B.

Change to smaller needle.

Rows 229 and 230: Rep Row 116—37 sts,

Cut B, join D.

Rows 231–234: Rep Row 116—33 sts.

Cut D, join B.

Rows 235 and 236: Rep Row 116—31 sts.

Cut B, join A.

Row 237: Rep Row 116—30 sts.

Change to larger needle.

Rows 238–261: [Rep Rows 158–161] 6 times—6 sts.

Row 262: K2, k2tog, k2—5 sts.

Row 263: K2, k2tog, k1—4 sts.

Row 264: K1, k2tog, k1—3 sts.

Row 265: K3tog.

Cut yarn and pull through.

Block afghan to measure 52 x 75 inches. ●

Fireside Comfort Afghan

Even when the cool air is nipping at your toes, you'll have this afghan to keep you warm. Choose three colors of worsted-weight yarn for your own tweedy look.

Design by Frances Hughes

· ·

Skill Level

◼◻◻◻ BEGINNER

Finished Size
Approx 52 x 60 inches

Materials
· Worsted weight yarn (228 yds/ 100g per skein): 5 skeins each red (A) and blue (B), 9 skeins variegated red/blue (C)
· Size 17 (12.75mm) circular needle or size needed to obtain gauge
· Size P/15/10mm crochet hook

Gauge
8 sts and 12 rows = 4 inches/10cm in St st with 4 strands held tog.

To save time, take time to check gauge.

Pattern Note
Circular needle is used to accommodate stitches; do not join, work back and forth in rows.

Afghan
Holding 1 strand each of A and B, and 2 strands C tog throughout, cast on 75 sts.

Row 1: K1, *p1, k1; rep from * across.

Rows 2 and 3: Rep Row 1.

Row 4: K1, p1, k1, knit to last 3 sts, k1, p1, k1.

Row 5: K1, p1, k1, purl to last 3 sts, k1, p1, k1.

Rows 6–23: [Rep Rows 4 and 5] 9 times.

Rows 24–45: [Rep Row 1] 22 times.

Rows 46–55: [Rep Rows 4 and 5] 5 times.

Rows 56–59: Rep Rows 1–4.

Row 60: K1, p1, k1, [k9, p3] 5 times, k9, k1, p1, k1.

Row 61: K1, p1, k1, [p9, k3] 5 times, p9, k1, p1, k1.

Rows 62–79: [Rep Rows 60 and 61] 9 times.

Rows 80–83: [Rep Row 1] 4 times.

Rows 84–93: [Rep Rows 4 and 5] 5 times.

Rows 94–115: [Rep Row 1] 22 times.

Rows 116–135: [Rep Rows 4 and 5] 10 times.

Rows 136–138: Rep Row 1.

Bind off all sts.

Edging
Rnd 1: With 4 strands held tog and crochet hook, attach yarn with a sc in any st, *ch 4, sk next st, sc in next st; rep from * around; join with sl st in joining sc.

Rnds 2–4: Sl st in ch-4 sp, ch 1, sc in same sp, *ch 4, sc in next ch-4 sp; rep from * around, join in first sc.

Fasten off. ●

Afghan-in-a-Minute

Big needles and two strands of yarn equal great results in this quick, beginner project.

Design by Diane Zangl

Skill Level

◨☐☐☐ BEGINNER

Finished Size
Approx 42 x 50 inches (blocked)

Materials
- Medium weight yarn (10-ply wool/
  poly-binder; 103 yds/50g per ball):
  8 balls green
- Light weight yarn (wool/mohair;
  114 yds/50g per ball): 8 balls celadon
- Size 15 (10mm) needles or size needed
  to obtain gauge

4 MEDIUM

3 LIGHT

Gauge
9 sts and 12 rows = 4 inches/10cm in St st.

To save time, take time to check gauge.

Pattern Note
Hold 1 strand of each yarn together throughout afghan. Slip first stitch of every row purlwise with yarn in front.

Afghan
With 2 strands held tog, cast on 90 sts.

Work in garter st for 7 rows.

Rows 1–12: Sl 1, k4, [k10, p10] 4 times, k5.

Rows 13–24: Sl 1, k4, [p10, k10] 4 times, k5.

[Rep Rows 1–24] 6 times.

Knit 8 rows. Bind off.

Block. ●

Quick & Easy Afghan

Knit this afghan quickly to gift or keep; the pattern is easy to memorize!

Design by Ellen Edwards Drechsler

· ·

Skill Level

◼◼◻◻ EASY

Finished Size
45 inches long x 56 inches wide

Materials
• Plymouth Yarn Co. Baby Alpaca Grande (bulky weight; 100% baby alpaca; 110 yds/100g per skein): 16 skeins green #1285
• Size 10½ (6.5mm) circular needle or size needed to obtain gauge
• Stitch markers

Gauge
14 sts = 4 inches/10cm in pat.

To save time, take time to check gauge.

Pattern Note
Circular needle is used to accommodate large number of stitches; do not join, work back and forth in rows.

Afghan
Cast on 228 sts.

Knit 8 rows.

On next row, place markers to separate first and last 6 sts for borders.

Rows 1 and 3: K6, *k2, p1; rep from * to last 6 sts, k6.

Row 2: K6, *k1, p2; rep from * to last 6 sts, k6.

Row 4: Knit across.

Rep Rows 1–4 for pat until afghan measures approx 44 inches, ending with Row 4.

Knit 6 rows.

Bind off all sts. ●

Clear Skies

Use three strands of yarn held together to make this periwinkle blue afghan with its lovely openwork.

Design by George Shaheen

. . . .

Skill Level
◖■■■▭ INTERMEDIATE

Finished Size
52 x 72 inches

Materials
- Bernat Berella "4" (worsted weight; 100% acrylic; 216 yds/100g per ball): 22 balls true periwinkle blue #01142
- Size 19 (15mm) circular knitting needle or size needed to obtain gauge
- Tapestry needle

Gauge
7 sts = 4 inches/10cm in St st (knit 1 row, purl 1 row) with 3 strands of yarn held tog.

To save time, take time to check gauge.

Pattern Notes
Afghan is worked with 3 strands of yarn held together.

Circular needle is used to accommodate large number of stitches; do not join, work back and forth in rows.

Afghan
Cast on 93 sts.

Row 1 (RS): Knit across.

Row 2: K5, *p11, k7; rep from * 3 times, p11, k5.

Row 3: K1, p4, *[k2tog] twice, [yo, k1] 3 times, yo, [ssk] twice, p7; rep from * 3 times, [k2tog] twice, [yo, k1] 3 times, yo, [ssk] twice, p4, k1.

Row 4: K1, p4, *k11, p7; rep from * 3 times, k11, p4, k1.

Row 5: Rep Row 2.

Rep Rows 2–5 until afghan measures 72 inches, ending by working a Row 5.

Note: When measuring, be sure afghan is flat and not stretched from weight of fabric.

Bind off as follows: K5, *p11, k7; rep from * 3 times, p11, k5. ●

Red Ridges Throw

A ridge pattern adds interesting texture to this classic afghan, stitched up in eye-popping red.

Design by Premier Yarns Design Team

. . . .

Skill Level

■■□□ EASY

Finished Size
41 x 60 inches

Materials
• Premier Yarns/Deborah Norville Collection Everyday Soft Worsted Solids (worsted weight; 100% acrylic; 203 yds/4 oz per ball): 8 balls really red #ED100-07
• Size 8 (5mm) 29-inch circular needle or size needed to obtain gauge
• Stitch markers

Gauge
17 sts and 24 rows = 4 inches in pat.

To save time, take time to check gauge.

Pattern Stitch
Ridge (multiple of 6 sts + 3)
Row 1 (RS): *K1, sl 1 wyif, k1, p3; rep from * to last 3 sts, k1, sl 1 wyif, k1.
Row 2: P3, *k3, p3; rep from * to end.
Row 3: *Sl 1 wyif, k1, sl 1 wyif, p3; rep from * to last 3 sts, sl 1 wyif, k1, sl 1 wyif.
Row 4: Rep Row 2.
Rep Rows 1–4 for pat.

Pattern Notes
Circular needle is used to accommodate large number of stitches; do not join, work back and forth in rows.

Slip all stitches purlwise.

Throw
Cast on 175 sts.

Work in garter st (knit every row) for 2 inches.

Row 1 (RS): K8, place marker, work Row 1 of Ridge pat to last 8 sts, place marker, k8.

Row 2: K8, work Row 2 of Ridge pat to last 8 sts, k8.

Continue as established, maintaining an 8-st garter st border on each edge and rep Rows 1–4 of Ridge pat over center 159 sts until piece measures 58 inches.

Work in garter st for 2 inches.

Bind off.

Finishing
Weave in ends. Block to finished measurements. ●

Heather Glen

This easy-to-knit afghan has that Irish feeling thanks to the Aran yarn and heather stripes.

Design by Ann E. Smith

Skill Level
■■□□ EASY

Finished Size
Approx 42 x 52 inches

Materials
- Worsted weight yarn (75% acrylic/ 25% wool; 210 yds/100g per skein): 10 skeins aran (MC), 4 skeins forest heather (A), 2 skeins pale forest heather (B)

4 MEDIUM

- Size 13 (9mm) circular needle or size needed to obtain gauge

Gauge
12 sts = 4 inches/10cm in pat with 2 strands of yarn held tog.

To save time, take time to check gauge.

Pattern Notes
Project uses 2 strands of yarn held together throughout.

Slip all stitches purlwise with yarn on wrong side of fabric.

Circular needle is used to accommodate the large number of stitches, do not join, work back and forth in rows.

Pattern Stitches
Body Pattern
Row 1 (RS): K2, [sl 1, k1] across to last 3 sts, end last rep sl 1, k2.
Row 2: P1, [k1, p1] across.
Row 3: K1, [sl 1, k1] across.
Row 4: K1, [p1, k1] across.
Rep Rows 1–4 for pat.

Box Pattern
Row 1 (RS): With B, k4, sl 1, [k3, sl 1] across to last 4 sts, end k4.

Row 2: With B, k4, sl 1, [k3, sl 1] across to last 4 sts, end k4.
Row 3: With MC, k1, [sl 1, k1] across.
Row 4: With MC, k1, [sl 1, k1] across.
Rep Rows 1–4 for pat.

Afghan
Beg at lower edge with A, cast on 125 sts.

First Border
Rows 1–12: With A, rep Rows 1–4 of Body pat.

Rows 13–16: With MC, rep Rows 1–4 of Body pat.

Rows 17–28: With B, rep Rows 1–4 of Body pat.

Rows 29–32: With MC, rep Rows 1–4 of Body pat.

Rows 33–44: With A, rep Rows 1–4 of Body pat.

Rows 45–56: With MC, rep Rows 1–4 of Body pat.

Box Stripe
Rows 1–8: Rep [Rows 1–4 of Box pat] twice.

Rows 9–20: With MC, rep [Rows 1–4 of Body pat] 3 times.

Rows 21–28: With A, rep [Rows 1–4 of Box pat] twice.

Rows 29–40: With MC, rep [Rows 1–4 of Body pat] 3 times.

Rows 41–48: With B, rep [Rows 1–4 of Box pat] twice.

Body
With MC, rep Body pat Rows 1–4 until piece measures approx 36½ inches from beg, ending with Row 4.

Rep Box Stripe Rows 1–48.

Second Border
Rows 1–12: With MC, rep First Border Rows 45–56.

Rows 13–56: Rep First Border Rows 1–44.

With A, loosely bind off kwise. ●

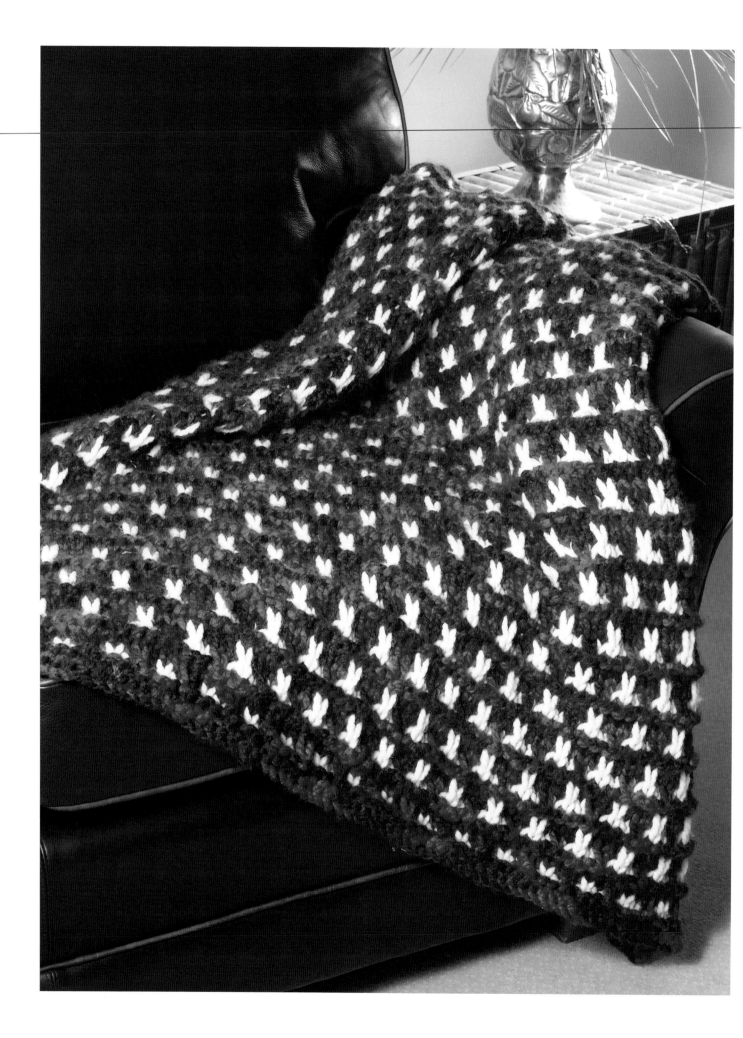

Tiffany Afghan

Everyone will love this warm, wonderful afghan. You'll appreciate how quickly it knits up!

Design by Kathleen Power Johnson

Skill Level
■□□□ BEGINNER

Finished Size
Approx 45 x 55 inches

Materials
- Lion Brand Yarn Jiffy Thick & Quick (super bulky weight; 100% acrylic; 84 yds/140g per ball): 9 balls Ozarks #210 (MC)
- Lion Brand Yarn Wool-Ease Thick & Quick (super bulky weight; 80% acrylic/20% wool; 106 yds/170g per ball): 3 balls fisherman #099 (CC)
- Size 17 (12.75mm) 36-inch circular needle or size needed to obtain gauge

6 SUPER BULKY

Gauge
8 sts and 10 rows = 4 inches/10cm in St st.

To save time, take time to check gauge.

Pattern Note
Circular needle is used to accommodate large number of stitches; do not join, work back and forth in rows.

Afghan
With MC, loosely cast on 85 sts.

Knit 3 rows.

Row 1 (RS): With CC, k2, *sl 1 wyib, k3; rep from *, end sl 1, k2.

Row 2: With CC, p2, *sl 1 wyif, p3; rep from *, end sl 1, p2.

Row 3: With MC, k4, *sl 1 wyib, k3; rep from *, end sl 1, k4.

Row 4: With MC, p4, *sl 1 wyif, p3; rep from *, end sl 1, p4.

Rows 5 and 6: With MC, knit.

Row 7: With CC, k4, *sl 1 wyib, k3; rep from *, end sl 1, k4.

Row 8: With CC, p4, *sl 1 wyif, p3; rep from *, end sl 1, p4.

Row 9: With MC, k2, *sl 1 wyib, k3; rep from *, end sl 1, k2.

Row 10: With MC, p2, *sl 1 wyif, p3; rep from *, end sl 1, p2.

Rows 11 and 12: Knit.

Rep Rows 1–12 of pat until afghan measures approx 55 inches, ending with Row 6 or 12.

Knit 1 row.

Bind off loosely.

Finishing
With RS facing, pick up and knit 104 sts along long edge. Knit 3 rows.

Bind off all sts.

Rep for opposite side. ●

Weekend Cabin

Navy and grays combine quite handsomely in this afghan, perfect for any room in the home, cabin or cottage.

Design by George Shaheen

. . . .

Skill Level
■ ■ ■ ☐ INTERMEDIATE

Finished Size
46 x 60 inches

Materials
- Red Heart Super Saver (worsted weight; 100% acrylic; 364 yds/198g per skein): 4 skeins each Windsor blue #380 (A), gray heather #400 (B), light gray #341 (C)
- Size 17 (12.75mm) circular knitting needle or size needed to obtain gauge
- Tapestry needle

Gauge
18 sts = 10 inches/25cm in garter st (knit every row) with 3 strands of yarn held tog.

To save time, take time to check gauge.

Pattern Notes
Afghan is worked with 3 strands of yarn held together.

Circular needle is used to accommodate large num- ber of stitches; do not join, work back and forth in rows.

Slip stitches purlwise with yarn in back.

Number of stitches will vary from row to row.

Afghan
With A, loosely cast on 81 sts.

Rows 1–3: Knit.

Row 4: K1, yo, sl 1, *k5, yo, sl 1; rep from * 12 times, k1—95 sts.

Row 5: K2, sl 1 (yo from previous row), *k6, sl 1 (yo from previous row); rep from * 12 times, k1.

Row 6: K1, k2tog, *yo, sl 1, k3, yo, sl 1, k2tog; rep from * 12 times, k1—107 sts.

Row 7: K2, *k1, sl 1 (yo from previous row), k4, sl 1 (yo from previous row), k1; rep from * 12 times, k1.

Row 8: K1, yo, sl 1, *k2tog, yo, sl 1, k1, yo, sl 1, k2tog, yo, sl 1; rep from * 12 times, k1—121 sts.

Row 9: K2, sl 1 (yo from previous row), *k2, sl 1 (yo from previous row); rep from * to last st, k1.

Row 10: K1, k2tog, *yo, sl 1, k2tog; rep from * to last st, k1—120 sts.

Row 11: K1, *k2, sl 1 (yo from previous row); rep from * to last 2 sts, k2.

Row 12: K2, *[k2tog, yo, sl 1] twice, k2tog, k1; rep from * 12 times, k1—107 sts.

Row 13: K2, *[k2, sl 1 (yo from previous row)] twice, k2; rep from * 12 times, k1.

Row 14: K2, *k1, k2tog, yo, sl 1, k2tog, k2; rep from * 12 times, k1—94 sts.

Row 15: K2, *k3, sl 1 (yo from previous row), k3; rep from * 12 times, k1.

Row 16: K2, *k3, k2tog, k2; rep from * 12 times, k1—81 sts.

Rows 17 and 18: Knit.

Rows 19–216: Rep Rows 1–18 in the following color sequence:

18 rows B, 18 rows C, 18 rows A, 18 rows B, 18 rows C, 18 rows A, 18 rows B, 18 rows C, 18 rows A, 18 rows B, 18 rows C

Bind off loosely. ●

Embossed Diamonds

A chunky, embossed diamond pattern adds to the rich appeal of this classically styled afghan.

Design by George Shaheen

Finished Size
40 x 55 inches

Materials
- Red Heart Super Saver (worsted weight; 100% acrylic; 364 yds/ 198g per skein): 7 skeins buff #334
- Size 17 (12.75mm) circular knitting needle or size needed to obtain gauge
- Tapestry needle

Gauge
19 sts = 10 inches/25cm in garter st (knit every row) with 3 strands of yarn held tog.

To save time, take time to check gauge.

Pattern Notes
Throw is worked with 3 strands of yarn held together.

Circular needle is used to accommodate large number of stitches; do not join, work back and forth in rows.

Due to nature of pattern, finished throw will not be a perfect rectangle and will need to be blocked to given measurements. Knitted fabric tends to shrink horizontally.

Afghan
Cast on 91 sts.

Row 1 (RS): K3, *p2, k2, p1, k3, p1, k1, p1, k3, p1, k2, p2, k3; rep from * 3 times.

Row 2: K1, p1, *p1, k2, p2, k5, p1, k5, p2, k2, p2; rep from * 3 times, k1.

Rows 3 and 4: Rep Rows 1 and 2.

Row 5: K2, *p2, k2, [p1, k3] 3 times, p1, k2, p2, k1; rep from * 3 times, k1.

Row 6: K1, p1, *k2, p2, k5, p3, k5, p2, k2, p1; rep from * 3 times, k1.

Rows 7 and 8: Rep Rows 5 and 6.

Row 9: K1, p1, *p1, k2, p1, k3, [p1, k2] twice, p1, k3, p1, k2, p2; rep from * 3 times, k1.

Row 10: K3, *p2, k5, p2, k1, p2, k5, p2, k3; rep from * 3 times.

Rows 11 and 12: Rep Rows 9 and 10.

Row 13: K1, p1, *k2, p1, k3, p1, k2, p3, k2, p1, k3, p1, k2, p1; rep from * 3 times, k1.

Row 14: K2, *p2, k5, p2, k3, p2, k5, p2, k1; rep from * 3 times, k1.

Rows 15 and 16: Rep Rows 13 and 14.

Row 17: K3, *p1, k3, p1, k2, p2, k1, p2, k2, p1, k3, p1, k3; rep from * 3 times.

Row 18: K1, p1, *p1, k5, p2, k2, p1, k2, p2, k5, p2; rep from * 3 times, k1.

Rows 19 and 20: Rep Rows 17 and 18.

Row 21: K2, *p1, k3, p1, k2, p2, k3, p2, k2, p1, k3, p1, k1; rep from * 3 times, k1.

Row 22: K1, p1, *k5, p2, k2, p3, k2, p2, k5, p1; rep from * 3 times, k1.

Rows 23 and 24: Rep Rows 21 and 22.

Row 25: K3, *p1, k3, p1, k2, p2, k1, p2, k2, p1, k3, p1, k3; rep from * 3 times.

Row 26: K1, p1, *p1, k5, p2, k2, p1, k2, p2, k5, p2; rep from * 3 times, k1.

Rows 27 and 28: Rep Rows 25 and 26.

Row 29: K1, p1, *k2, p1, k3, p1, k2, p3, k2, p1, k3, p1, k2, p1; rep from * 3 times, k1.

Row 30: K2, *p2, k5, p2, k3, p2, k5, p2, k1; rep from * 3 times, k1.

Rows 31 and 32: Rep Rows 29 and 30.

Row 33: K1, p1, *p1, k2, p1, k3, [p1, k2] twice, p1, k3, p1, k2, p2; rep from * 3 times, k1.

Row 34: K3, *p2, k5, p2, k1, p2, k5, p2, k3; rep from * 3 times.

Rows 35 and 36: Rep Rows 33 and 34.

Row 37: K2, *p2, k2, [p1, k3] 3 times, p1, k2, p2, k1; rep from * 3 times, k1.

Row 38: K1, p1, *k2, p2, k5, p3, k5, p2, k2, p1; rep from * 3 times, k1.

Rows 39 and 40: Rep Rows 37 and 38.

Rep Rows 1–40 until afghan measures about 55 inches, ending by working an even-numbered row.

Note: When measuring, be sure afghan is flat and not stretched from weight of fabric.

Bind off working next row of pat.

Block throw to measure 40 x 55 inches. ●

On the Fringes

Drape your favorite armchair in luxury with this collection of afghans adorned with a variety of fringed and tasseled accents. You'll add a fanciful feel to your decor by showcasing one of these impressive creations.

Twisting Cables

Spectacular twisting cables and double fringe look especially pretty in pink.

Design by Kathy Wesley

. . . .

Skill Level

⬛⬛⬛⬜ INTERMEDIATE

Finished Size
Approx 42 x 52 inches

Materials

- Worsted weight yarn: 35 oz/ 2,450 yds/1,000g pink
- Size 10 (6mm) 29-inch circular knitting needle or size needed to obtain gauge
- Cable needle

Gauge
16 sts and 24 rows = 4 inches/10cm in St st.

To save time, take time to check gauge.

Pattern Stitch
Cable Front (CF): Slip next 3 sts onto cn and hold in front of work, K4, K3 sts from cn.

Lower Border
Cast on 197 sts.

Row 1 (RS): Knit.

Row 2: Knit.

Row 3: K1, p1, k1-tbl, *p4, k7, p4, k1-tbl; rep from * 11 times more, p1, k1.

Row 4: K2, p1-tbl, *k4, p7, k4, p1-tbl; rep from * 11 times more, k2.

Row 5: K1, p1, knit in front, in back, and in front of next st, *p4, k7, p4, knit in front, in back and in front of next st; rep from * 11 times more, p1, k1.

Row 6: K2, p3 tog, *k4, p7, k4, p3tog; rep from * 11 times more, k2.

Rows 7–10: Rep Rows 3–6.

Body
Row 1: K1, p1, k1-tbl, p4, *CF, p4, k1-tbl, p4; rep from * 10 times more, CF, p4, k1-tbl, p1, k1.

Row 2: K2, p1-tbl, k4, *p7, k4, p1-tbl, k4; rep from * 10 times more, p7, k4, p1-tbl, k2.

Row 3: K1, p1, knit in front, in back, and in front of next st, p4, *†k2tog, yo, k1, p1, k1, yo, ssk, p4, knit in front, in back, and in front of next st†; p4; rep from * 10 times more, then rep from † to † once, p1, k1.

Row 4: K2, p3tog, k4, *p7, k4, p3tog, k4; rep from * 10 times more, p7, k4, p3tog, k2.

Row 5: K1, p1, k1-tbl, p4, *k3, p1, k3, p4, k1-tbl, p4; rep from * 10 times more, k3, p1, k3, p4, k1-tbl, p1, k1.

Row 6: K2, p1-tbl, k4, *p7, k4, p1-tbl, k4; rep from * 10 times more, p7, k4, p1-tbl, k2.

Rows 7–18: [Rep Rows 3–6] 3 times more.

Row 19: K1, p1, knit in front, in back and in front of next st, p4, *CF, p4, knit in front, in back, and in front of next st; p4; rep from * 10 times more, CF; p4, knit in front, in back and in front of next st, p1, k1.

Row 20: K2, p3tog, k4, *p7, k4, p3tog, k4; rep from * 10 times more, p7, k4, p3tog, k2.

Row 21: K1, p1, k1-tbl, p4, *k7, p4, k1-tbl, p4; rep from * 10 times more, k7, p4, k1-tbl, p1, k1.

Row 22: K2, p1-tbl, k4, *p7, k4, p1-tbl, k4; rep from * 10 times more, p7, k4, p1-tbl, k2.

Row 23: K1, p1, knit in front, in back and in front of next s, p4, *k7, p4, knit in front, in back and in front of next st, p4; rep from * 10 times more; k7, p4, knit in front, in back and in front of next st, p1, k1.

Row 24: K2, p3tog, k4, *p7, k4, p3tog, k4; rep from * 10 times more; p7, k4, p3tog, k2.

Row 25: K1, p1, k1-tbl, p4, * CF, p4, k1-tbl, p4; rep from * 10 times more, CF, p4, k1-tbl, p1, k1.

Row 26: K2, p1-tbl, k4, *p7, k4, p1-tbl, k4; rep from * 10 times more, p7, k4, p1-tbl, k2.

Rep Rows 3–26 until piece measures approx 45 inches from cast-on edge.

Rep Rows 3–20.

Upper Border
[Rep Rows 3–6 of lower border] twice.

Next row: Knit.

Bind off.

Fringe
Following Fringe instructions on page 126, make double-knot fringe. Cut 30-inch strands of yarn; use 8 strands for each knot. Tie knots evenly spaced (approx every 5 sts) across each short end of afghan. Trim ends even. ●

California Sunset

Use your scrap yarns to create the chains on this double-fringed afghan.

Design by Sandy Scoville

. . . .

Skill Level
■■□□ EASY

Finished Size
Approx 44 x 60 inches (excluding fringe)

Materials
- Worsted weight yarn: 28 oz/1,9?? yds/ 840g main color (MC), 3½ oz/ 245 yds/105g each of 6 different scrap colors
- Size 8 (5mm) 29-inch circular knitting needle
- Size H/8 (5mm) crochet hook (for edging)

Gauge
16 sts = 4 inches/10cm in St st.

To save time, take time to check gauge.

Afghan
Notes: Slip all sts as to purl. Carry MC loosely along side edge when not in use.

With MC, cast on 182 sts.

Row 1 (RS): Knit.

Row 2: Purl.

Rows 3 and 4: With any scrap color, knit.

Row 5: With MC, k6, *sl 2, k6; rep from * across.

Row 6: P6, *sl 2, p6; rep from * across.

Row 7: With same scrap color, k6, *sl 2, k6; rep from * across.

Row 8: Knit.

Rows 9 and 10: With MC, rep Rows 1 and 2.

Rows 11 and 12: With new scrap color, knit.

Row 13: With MC, k2, sl 2, *k6, sl 2; rep from * to last 2 sts, k2.

Row 14: P2, sl 2, *p6, sl 2; rep from * to last 2 sts; p2.

Row 15: With same scrap color, k2, sl 2, *k6, sl 2; rep from * to last 2 sts, k2.

Row 16: Knit.

Rep Rows 1–16 until afghan measures about 60 inches, ending by working a Row 2.

Knit 1 row.

Bind off as to purl.

Border
Hold afghan with RS facing you and 1 short side at top; with crochet hook and MC, make slip knot on hook and join with an sc in first row in upper RH corner.

Rnd 1: 2 sc in same sp as joining—beg corner made; working across side, sc in each st to last st; 3 sc in next st—corner made; working along next side in ends of rows, work 2 sc for every 3 rows to next side; working across next side, 3 sc in first st—corner made; sc in each st to last st; 3 sc in next st—corner made; working along next side in ends of rows, work same number of sc as on opposite side; join in joining sc.

Rnd 2: Ch 1, sc in same sc as joining; 3 sc in next sc—corner made; *sc in each sc to 2nd sc of next corner; 3 sc in next sc; rep from * twice more; sc in each sc to first sc; join in first sc.

Bind off.

Fringe
Following Fringe instructions on page 126, make double-knot fringe. Cut 24-inch strands of MC. For each knot use 6 strands. Tie knots evenly spaced (about every 5th st) across each short end of afghan. Tie 2nd row of knots using half the strands of each of 2 adjoining knots to make a knot.

Trim ends even. ●

Subtle Chevron

Easy to make—just knit strips, sew them together and add luxuriously long fringe.

Design by Kathy Wesley

· ·

Skill Level
■■□□ EASY

Finished Size
Approx 40 x 54 inches

Materials
- Worsted weight yarn: 21 oz/1,470 yds/ 630g main color (MC) 4 oz/ 280 yds/120g each 2 colors (A), (B), 3½ oz/245 yds/105g each or 4 different scrap colors
- Size 8 (5mm) knitting needles

Gauge
16 sts = 4 inches/10 cm in St st.

To save time, take time to check gauge.

Right-Hand Strip
Make 1

With A, cast on 21 sts.

Row 1 (RS): K4, [k2, p2] twice; k1, [p2, k2] twice.

Row 2: P1, k2, p2, k2, p3, k2, p2, k2, p1, k4.

Row 3: K5, p1, k2, p2, k5, p2, k2, p1, k1.

Row 4: P3, k2, p2, k1, p1, k1, p2, k2, p3, k4.

Rep Rows 1–4 until strip measures about 54 inches, ending by working a Row 4.

Bind off.

Left-Hand Strip
Make 1

With B, cast on 21 sts.

Row 1 (RS): [K2, p2] twice; k1, [p2, k2] twice; k4.

Row 2: K4, p1, k2, p2, k2, p3, k2, p2, k2, p1.

Row 3: K1, p1, k2, p2, k5, p2, k2, p1, k5.

Row 4: K4, p3, k2, p2, k1, p1, k1, p2, k2, p3.

Rep Rows 1–4 until strip has same number of reps as Right-Hand Strip.

Bind off.

Center Strips
Make 5 MC & 1 each of 4 scrap colors

Cast on 17 sts.

Row 1: [K2, p2] twice; k1, [p2, k2] twice.

Row 2: P1, k2, p2, k2, p3, k2, p2, k2, p1.

Row 3: K1, p1, k2, p2, k5, p2, k2, p1, k1.

Row 4: P3, k2, p2, k1, p1, k1, p2, k2, p3.

Rep Rows 1–4 until strip has same number of reps as Right-Hand Strip.

Bind off.

Assembly
Alternate MC and scrap-color Center strips between Right-Hand and Left-Hand strips. Sew strips tog.

Fringe
Following Fringe instructions on page 126, make single-knot fringe. Cut 20-inch strands of MC. For each knot use 10 strands. Tie knots evenly spaced at each edge, each seam and in center of each strip across each short end of afghan.

Trim ends even. ●

Diamonds Are for Cuddling

Made with super bulky-weight yarn, this quickie afghan features a captivating diamond stitch pattern and has a definite touch of class!

Design by Kathleen Power Johnson

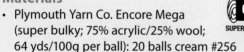

Skill Level
■■■□ INTERMEDIATE

Finished Size
Approx 51 x 60 inches (excluding fringe)

Materials
- Plymouth Yarn Co. Encore Mega (super bulky; 75% acrylic/25% wool; 64 yds/100g per ball): 20 balls cream #256
- Size 15 (10mm) 29-inch circular needle or size needed to obtain gauge
- Size K/10½ (6.5mm) crochet hook (for fringe)

6 SUPER BULKY

Gauge
8 sts and 12 rows = 4 inches/10cm in St st.

To save time, take time to check gauge.

Pattern Notes
Circular needle is used to accommodate stitches; do not join, work back and forth in rows.

Always knit first and last stitch of every row (edge stitches).

Chart is provided for those preferring to work pattern from a chart. Only right side rows are shown.

Afghan
Loosely cast on 102 sts.

Knit 2 rows. Work in St st (knit 1 row, purl 1 row) for 4 inches.

Beg Pat
Row 1 (RS): K3, *k1, [yo, ssk] 5 times, k1; rep from * to last 3 sts, end k3.

Row 2 and all WS rows: K1, purl to last st, k1.

Row 3: K3, *k2, [yo, ssk] 4 times, k2; rep from * to last 3 sts, end k3.

Row 5: K6, [yo, ssk] 3 times, k2, yo, *ssk, k2, [yo, ssk] 3 times, k2, yo; rep from * to last 4 sts, end ssk, k2.

Row 7: K3, *yo, ssk, k2, [yo, ssk] twice, k2, yo, ssk; rep from * to last 3 sts, end k3.

Row 9: K2, [k2, yo, ssk] 3 times, yo, *ssk, [yo, ssk, k2] twice, yo, ssk, yo; rep from * to last 4 sts, end ssk, k2.

Row 11: K3, *[yo, ssk] twice, k4, [yo, ssk] twice; rep from * to last 3 sts, end k3.

Row 13: K4, [yo, ssk] twice, k2, [yo, ssk] twice, yo, *[ssk, yo] twice, ssk, k2, [yo, ssk] twice, yo; rep from * to last 4 sts, end ssk, k2.

Row 15: Rep Row 11.

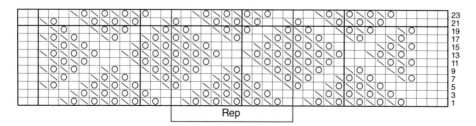

			STITCH KEY
			□ Knit
			⊙ Yo
			◹ Ssk

DIAMOND CHART

Note: Only RS rows are shown.

Row 17: Rep Row 9.

Row 19: Rep Row 7.

Row 21: Rep Row 5.

Row 23: Rep Row 3.

Row 24: K1, purl to last st, k1.

Rep Rows 1–24 until afghan measures approx 52 inches, ending with Row 24.

Beg with a knit row, work in St st for 3½ inches, ending with a RS row. Knit 2 rows.

Bind off all sts.

Fringe
Make spaghetti-style fringe referring to page 126.
Cut 51 (17-inch) lengths of yarn. Use 1 strand for each knot. Tie knot in every other st of purl ridge across each short end. Trim ends even. ●

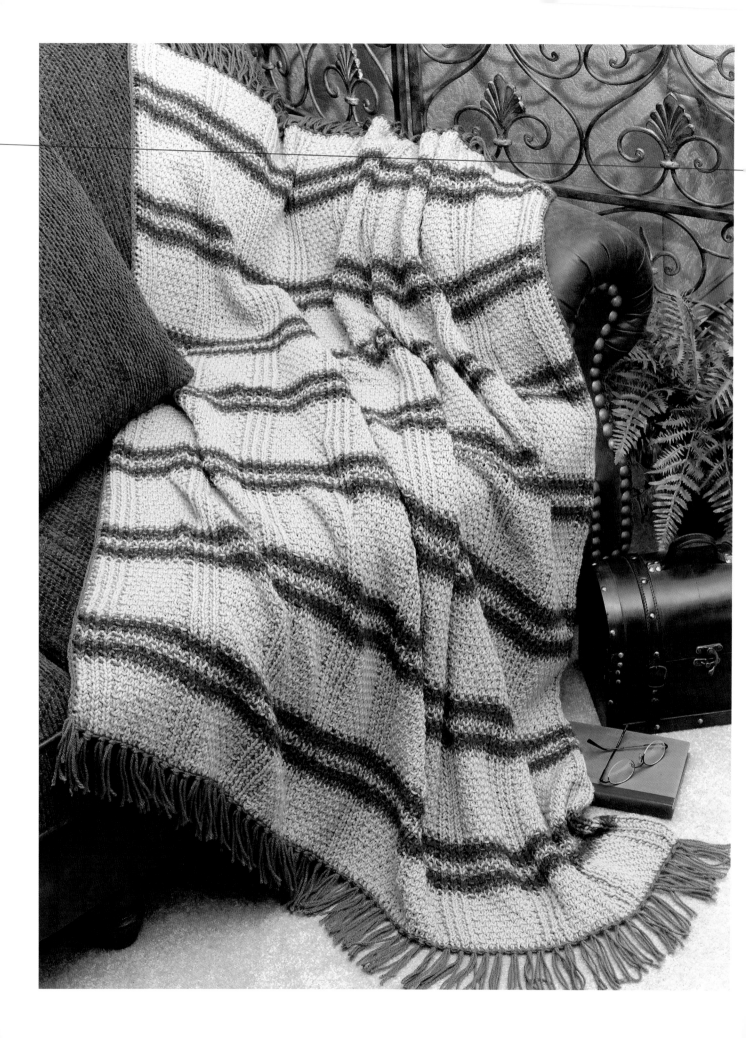

Woven-Look Throw

Beautiful thyme greens are spruced up with red stripes to create this delightful woven-look throw.

Design by Carolyn Pfeifer

Skill Level
■■□□ EASY

Finished Size
Approx 47 x 55 inches

Materials
- Worsted weight yarn (100% acrylic; 364 yds/198g per skein): 4 skeins light sage (A), 2 skeins each medium sage (B) and dark red (C)
- Size 11 (8mm) 24-inch circular needle or size needed to obtain gauge
- Size H/8 (5mm) crochet hook (optional, for edging)

Gauge
16 sts and 20 rows = 4 inches/10cm.

To save time, take time to check gauge.

Afghan
With A, cast on 180 sts.

Row 1 (RS): Sl 1kwise, *p1, [k1, p1] 3 times, [wyif, sl 1pwise, wyib, k1] 6 times; rep from * 8 times more, p1, [k1, p1] 3 times, k1.

Row 2: Sl 1kwise, purl across to last st, k1.

Row 3: Sl 1kwise, *p1, [k1, p1] 3 times, [k1, wyif, sl 1pwise] 6 times; rep from * 8 times more, p1, [k1, p1] 3 times, k1.

Row 4: Rep Row 2.

Rows 5–16: [Rep Rows 1–4] 3 times more.

Rows 17 and 18: With B, rep Rows 1 and 2.

Rows 19 and 20: With C, rep Rows 3 and 4.

Rows 21 and 22: With B, rep Rows 1 and 2.

Rows 23 and 24: With A, rep Rows 3 and 4.

Rows 25 and 26: With B, rep Rows 1 and 2.

Rows 27 and 28: With C, rep Rows 3 and 4.

Rows 29 and 30: With B, rep Rows 1 and 2.

Rows 31 and 32: With A, rep Rows 3 and 4.

Continue to rep Rows 1–4 in the following color sequence:

*18 rows A, 2 rows B, 2 rows C, 2 rows B, 2 rows A, 2 rows B, 2 rows C, 2 rows B, 2 rows A.

Rep from * 5 times more.

Continue in pat with A for 14 rows.

Bind off kwise.

Edging
Note: As this afghan tends to be loose and stretchy, it is suggested that a crocheted edging be added to hold edges firm.

Hold afghan with cast-on edge at top, attach B in upper RH corner, *sc in next 3 sts, sk next st, rep from * to next corner, ch 1, working along side edge, loosely sc in end of every other row to next corner, ch 1, **sc in next 3 sts, sk next st, rep from ** to next corner, working along next side edge, loosely sc in end of every other row to first sc, ch 1, join with sl st in first sc.

Fasten off.

Fringe
Make single-knot fringe referring to Fringe instructions on page 126. Cut 9-inch lengths of B. Use 2 strands for each knot, tie knots in every other st across each short end.

Trim ends even.

Steam lightly. ●

High-Flying Colors

This afghan is knit with a main color and fifteen different scrap colors to create a design that would brighten anyone's day.

Design by Sandy Scoville

Skill Level
■■□□ EASY

Finished Size
Approx 44 x 60 inches (excluding fringe)

Materials
- Worsted weight yarn: 18 oz/1,260 yds/ 540g main color (MC), 2½ oz/ 175 yds/75g each of 15 scrap colors
- Size 9 (5.5mm) 29-inch circular knitting needle

Gauge
18 sts = 4 inches/10cm in St st.

To save time, take time to check gauge.

Pattern Notes
Circular needle used to accommodate stitches; do not join, work back and forth in rows.

Slip all stitches purlwise.

Do not carry unused colors.

Afghan
With MC, cast on 206 sts.

Bottom Border
Row 1 (RS): Knit.

Rows 2–4: Rep Row 1.

Body
Row 1 (RS): With scrap color, k1, *sl 2, k4; rep from * to last st, k1.

Row 2: P1, k2, p2, *sl 2, wyib, k2, p2; rep from * to last 3 sts, sl 2, p1.

Row 3: With new scrap color, k3, sl 2, *k4, sl 2; rep from * to last 3 sts, k3.

Row 4: P3, sl 2, wyib, k2, *p2, sl 2, wyib, k2; rep from * to last st, p1.

Row 5: With new scrap color, k5, sl 2, *k4, sl 2; rep from * to last st, k1.

Row 6: P1, *sl 2, wyib, k2, p2; rep from * to last st, p1.

Rows 7 and 8: With MC, rep Rows 1 and 2.

Rows 9 and 10: With new scrap color, rep Rows 3 and 4.

Rows 11 and 12: With new scrap color, rep Rows 5 and 6.

Rows 13 and 14: With new scrap color, rep Rows 1 and 2.

Rows 15 and 16: With MC, rep Rows 3 and 4.

Rows 17 and 18: With new scrap color, rep Rows 5 and 6.

Rows 19 and 20: With new scrap color, rep Rows 1 and 2.

Rows 21 and 22: With new scrap color, rep Rows 3 and 4.

Rows 23 and 24: With MC, rep Rows 5 and 6.

Rep Rows 1–24 until afghan measures about 58 inches, ending by working any scrap color WS row.

Top Border
Row 1: With MC, knit.

Rows 2 and 3: Rep Row 1.

Bind off.

Side Border
Hold afghan with RS facing you and 1 long side at top; with MC, pick up 275 sts evenly spaced across side.

Row 1: Knit.

Rows 2–4: Rep Row 1.

Bind off.

Rep on other long side.

Fringe
Following Fringe instructions on page 126, make single-knot fringe. Cut 24-inch strands of MC. For each knot use 4 strands. Tie knots evenly spaced (about every 4th st) across each short end of afghan.

Trim ends even. ●

Sedona Reds Throw

With its rich color and texture, this project will make a warm impression.

Design by Cindy Adams

Gauge
14 sts = 4 inches/10cm in pat.

To save time, take time to check gauge.

Pattern Stitch
Twisted Rib (multiple of 6 sts)
Rows 1 and 3 (RS): *P2, k2, p2; rep from * across.
Rows 2 and 4: *K2, p2, k2; rep from * across.
Row 5: *Sl 2 sts to cn and hold in back, k1, p2 from cn, sl 1 st to cn and hold in front, p2, k1 from cn; rep from * across.
Rows 6, 8 and 10: *P1, k4, p1; rep from * across.
Rows 7 and 9: *K1, p4, k1; rep from * across.

Row 11: *Sl 1 st to cn and hold in front, p2, k1 from cn, sl 2 sts to cn and hold in back, k1, p2 from cn; rep from * across.
Row 12: *K2, p2, k2; rep from * across.
Rep Rows 1–12 for pat.

Pattern Notes
Circular needle is used to accommodate large number of stitches; do not join, work back and forth in rows.

On all rows, slip the first stitch with yarn in front, knit the last stitch. These edge stitches are not included in pattern stitch instructions.

Throw
Cast on 170 sts (168 sts + 2 edge sts).

Beg with Row 1, work in Twisted Rib pat until throw measures approx 60 inches, ending with Row 3.

Bind off all sts.

Fringe
Following Fringe instructions on page 126, make fringe. Cut 20-inch strands. Use 4 strands for each knot. Make 1 knot fringe at each corner and 1 in center of each k2 across ends. Trim even as needed. •

Rainbow Ladder

Seven different colors (get out your scrap yarn!) create a colorful ladder effect against the blue background.

Design by Sandy Scoville

· ·

Skill Level
■◧□□ EASY

Finished Size
Approx 42 x 60 inches (excluding fringe)

Materials
- Worsted weight yarn (210 yds/90g per skein): 10 skeins blue (MC) and 1 skein each of 7 different colors (CC)
- Size 8 (5mm) 29-inch circular knitting needle or size needed to obtain gauge

Gauge
20 sts = 4 inches/10cm in St st (knit 1 row, purl 1 row).

To save time, take time to check gauge.

Pattern Notes
Carry main color loosely along side edge when not in use. At beginning of row, bring the working color under the previous color to lock it in place.

Slip all stitches purlwise.

Afghan
With MC, cast on 188 sts.

Bottom Border
Row 1 (RS): Knit.

Rows 2–4: Rep Row 1.

Body
Row 1 (RS): With MC, knit.

Row 2: Purl.

Rows 3 and 4: Rep Rows 1 and 2.

Row 5: With any CC, k8; *sl 2 wyib, k8; rep from * across.

Row 6: K8; *sl 2 wyif, k8; rep from * across.

Row 7: P8; *sl 2 wyib, p8; rep from * across.

Row 8: Rep Row 6.

Rows 9–12: Rep Rows 1–4.

Rows 13–16: With new CC, rep Rows 5–8.

Rep Rows 1–8, changing to new CC on each Row 5, until afghan measures about 59 inches, ending by working a Row 4.

Top Border
Row 1 (RS): With MC, knit.

Rows 2–5: Rep Row 1.

Bind off.

Weave in all ends.

Fringe
Referring to Fringe instructions on page 126, make fringe. Cut 24-inch lengths of MC. For each knot use 8 strands. Tie knots evenly spaced (at each MC stripe and each corner) across each short end of afghan.

Trim ends even. ●

Richly Textured Afghan

Knit with big needles and bulky yarn, this afghan is a quick and easy project.

Design by Carolyn Pfeifer

. . . .

Skill Level
■□■□□ EASY

Finished Size
Approx 44 x 58 inches (excluding fringe)

Materials
- Lion Brand Yarn Homespun (bulky weight; 98% acrylic/ 2% polyester; 185 yds/170g per skein): 5 skeins waterfall #329 (A), 1 skein mixed berries #411 (B)
- Size 15 (10mm) 24-inch circular needle

Gauge
10 sts and 13 rows = 4 inches/10cm.

To save time, take time to check gauge.

Special Abbreviation
Knit in row Below Increase (K1B Inc): Knit into next st in row below needle; without removing st from LH needle, knit in back of same st, to inc 1 st.

Afghan
With A, cast on 121 sts.

Row 1 (RS): Sl 1kwise, knit across.

Row 2: Sl 1k, k1, sl 1p, k1, psso, K1B Inc, *k2, sl 1, k1, psso, K1B Inc; rep from * to last st, k1.

Rows 3–16: Rep Row 2.

Rows 17–20: With B, knit.

Rows 21–36: With A, rep Row 2.

[Rep Rows 17–36] 7 times more.

Bind off kwise.

Fringe
Make single-knot fringe referring to Fringe instructions on page 126. Cut 12-inch lengths of B. Using 8 strands for each knot, tie knots evenly spaced (about every 3 inches) across each short end of afghan.

Trim ends even. ●

Seaside Throw

With gorgeous yarn and a little time, you'll soon be enjoying this reversible throw.

Design by Scarlet Taylor

Skill Level
■□□□ BEGINNER

Finished Size
Approx 44 x 55 inches (excluding fringe)

Materials
- Bulky weight yarn (49 yds/ 50g per ball): 22 balls multicolored
- Size 13 (9mm) circular knitting needle or size needed to obtain gauge
- Large crochet hook (for fringe)

5 BULKY

Gauge
9 sts and 14 rows = 4 inches/10cm in k3, p3 rib.

To save time, take time to check gauge.

Pattern Note
Circular needle is used to accommodate large number of stitches; do not join, work back and forth in rows.

Throw

Loosely cast on 99 sts.

Row 1 (RS): K3, *p3, k3; rep from * across.

Row 2: P3, *k3, p3; rep from * across.

Rep Rows 1 and 2 until throw measures approx 55 inches from beg, ending with a WS row.

Bind off loosely in rib.

Block lightly if desired.

Fringe
Make single-knot fringe referring to Fringe instructions on page 126. Cut 14-inch strands for fringe. Use 3 strands for each knot; tie a knot at end of each k3 rib across RS of cast-on and bound-off edges. Trim ends even. ●

Ripple Effect

We offer many options on this time-favored technique. Ripple afghans
are easy to make and will add dimension and interest to your decor.

Springtime Ripples

Perfect for breezy spring days (or warmer climates any time of year), this cotton afghan is knit in colors that remind us of flowers and greenery.

Design by Melissa Leapman

Skill Level
◖■□□ EASY

Finished Size
Approx 46 x 56 inches

Materials
- Worsted weight yarn (100% cotton; 114 yds/2½ oz per ball): 7 balls light green (A), 11 balls variegated (B), 9 balls rose pink (C)
- Size 11 (8mm) circular needle
- Size 13 (9mm) circular needle or size needed to obtain gauge

4 MEDIUM

Gauge
12 sts and 15 rows = 4 inches/10cm with larger needle and 2 strands of yarn held tog.

To save time, take time to check gauge.

Pattern Stitch
Stripe
Work 10 rows A; *6 rows B, 2 rows A, 6 rows C, 2 rows A, rep from * for pat.

Pattern Notes
Project uses 2 strands of yarn held together throughout.

Circular needles are used to accommodate the large number of stitches; do not join, work back and forth in rows.

Throw
With smaller needle and 2 strands of A held tog, cast on 138 sts. Work 10 rows of garter st.

Change to larger needle.

Row 1 (RS): Knit.

Row 2: Purl.

Rows 3–6: Rep Rows 1 and 2.

Row 7: *[K2tog] 4 times, [yo, k1] 7 times; yo, [ssk] 4 times; rep from * across.

Row 8: Knit.

Rep Rows 1–8 in Stripe pat until throw measures approx 55 inches from beg, ending with Row 6 of pat.

Change to smaller needle and A, work 10 rows of garter st.

Bind off all sts. ●

Zigzag Eyelet Throw

This zigzag eyelet pattern is actually an easy pattern, perfect for knitters who want to create an impressive, yet easy, throw.

Design by Melissa Leapman

Skill Level

■■□□ EASY

Finished Size
Approx 40 x 50 inches

Materials
- Worsted weight yarn (100% cotton; 114 yds/2½ oz per ball): 17 balls yellow
- Size 11 (8mm) circular needle
- Size 13 (9mm) circular needle or size needed to obtain gauge
- Stitch markers

Gauge
12 sts and 16 rows = 4 inches/10cm with larger needle and 2 strands of yarn held tog.

To save time, take time to check gauge.

Pattern Notes
Project uses 2 strands of yarn held together throughout.

Circular needles are used to accommodate the large number of stitches; do not join, work back and forth in rows.

Throw
Border
With smaller needle and 2 strands of yarn held tog, cast on 120 sts.

Work 10 rows of garter st.

Change to larger needle.

Body
Row 1 (RS): K5, place marker, k7, *k2tog, yo, k8; rep from * across to last 8 sts, end k2tog, yo, k1, place marker, k5.

Row 2 and all WS rows: K5, purl across to last 5 sts, k5.

Row 3: K11, *k2tog, yo, k8; rep from * across to last 9 sts, end k2tog, yo, k7.

Row 5: K10, *k2tog, yo, k8; rep from * across to last 10 sts, end k2tog, yo, k8.

Row 7: K9, *k2tog, yo, k8; rep from * across to last 11 sts, end k2tog, yo, k9.

Row 9: K8, *k2tog, yo, k8; rep from * across to last 12 sts, end k2tog, yo, k10.

Row 11: K7, *k2tog, yo, k8; rep from * across to last 13 sts, end k2tog, yo, k11.

Row 13: K6, *k2tog, yo, k8; rep from * across to last 14 sts, end k2tog, yo, k12.

Row 15: K5, *k2tog, yo, k8; rep from * across to last 15 sts, end k2tog, yo, k13.

Row 17: K7, *yo, ssk, k8; rep from * across to last 13 sts, end yo, ssk, k11.

Row 19: K8, *yo, ssk, k8; rep from * across to last 12 sts, end yo, ssk, k10.

Row 21: K9, *yo, ssk, k8; rep from * across to last 11 sts, end yo, ssk, k9.

Row 23: K10, *yo, ssk, k8; rep from * across to last 10 sts, end yo, ssk, k8.

Row 25: K11, *yo, ssk, k8; rep from * across to last 9 sts, end yo, ssk, k7.

Row 27: K12, *yo, ssk, k8; rep from * across to last 8 sts, end yo, ssk, k6.

Row 29: K13, *yo, ssk, k8; rep from * across to last 7 sts, end yo, ssk, k5.

Row 30: K5, purl across to last 5 sts, k5.

Rep Rows 3–30 for pat until throw measures approx 49 inches from beg, ending with Row 16 of pat.

Border
Change to smaller needle and work 10 rows of garter st.

Bind off all sts. Block to measurements. ●

Sherbet Ripple Afghan

Ripple afghans are classic favorites, and this chunky style, worked using three strands of yarn together throughout, is warm and wonderful.

Design by Ann E. Smith

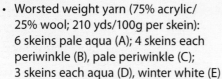

Skill Level
◼◼☐☐☐ EASY

Finished Size
Approx 42 x 57 inches

Materials
- Worsted weight yarn (75% acrylic/ 25% wool; 210 yds/100g per skein): 6 skeins pale aqua (A); 4 skeins each periwinkle (B), pale periwinkle (C); 3 skeins each aqua (D), winter white (E)
- Size 15 (10mm) circular needle or size needed to obtain gauge

4 MEDIUM

Gauge
10 sts and 14 rows = 4 inches/10cm in body pat with 3 strands of yarn held tog.

To save time, take time to check gauge.

Pattern Notes
Project uses 3 strands of yarn held together throughout.

To use 4th skeins of B and C, wind each skein into 3 separate balls.

Circular needle is used to accommodate the large number of stitches; do not join, work back and forth in rows.

Afghan
Beg at lower edge with D, cast on 105 sts.

Border
Row 1 (WS): Knit.

Row 2: K2, p101, k2.

Row 3: Knit.

Rows 4 and 5: Rep Rows 2 and 3. Cut D.

Body Pattern
Row 1 (RS): With A, k4, yo, k5, k3tog, k5, yo, *k1, yo, k5, k3tog, k5, yo; rep from * across to last 4 sts, end k4.

Row 2: K2, p101, k2.

Row 3: Rep Row 1.

Row 4: Knit.

Rows 5–8: Rep Rows 1–4.

Rows 9–11: Rep Rows 1–3.

Row 12: With B, k2, p101, k2.

Row 13: Rep Row 12.

Row 14: Knit.

Row 15: Rep Row 12.

Row 16: Knit.

Rows 17–27: With C, rep Rows 1–11.

Rows 28–32: With E, rep Rows 12–16.

Rows 33–43: With A, rep Rows 1–11.

Rows 44–48: With E, rep Rows 12–16.

Rows 49–59: With B, rep Rows 1–11.

Rows 60–64: With D, rep Rows 12–16.

Rows 65–176: Rep Rows 1–64 in color sequence as established, ending with Row 48.

Rows 177–187: With C, rep Rows 1–11.

Rows 188–192: With B, rep Rows 12–16.

Rows 193–203: With A, rep Rows 1–11.

Rows 204–208: With D, rep Rows 12–16.

With D, loosely bind off kwise. ●

Tiger Stripes

Wild and vibrant like a tiger's coat, the colors in this afghan create a beautiful blend that would liven up any decor.

Design by George Shaheen

. . . .

Skill Level
■■■□ INTERMEDIATE

Finished Size
42 x 56 inches

Materials

- Lion Brand Wool-Ease Chunky (bulky weight; 80% acrylic/20%wool; 153 yds/140g per skein): 5 skeins each spice #135 (A) and pumpkin #133 (B), 1 skein black #153 (C)
- Super bulky weight novelty yarn (39 yds/50g per ball): 3 balls multicolored (D)
- Size 35 (19mm) straight knitting needles, 14-inches long or size needed to obtain gauge
- Tapestry needle

Gauge
26 sts = 10 inches/25cm in pat st with 2 strands of yarn held tog.

To save time, take time to check gauge.

Special Abbreviation
Increase (inc): Purl into front and back of next st.

Pattern Note
Afghan is worked with 2 strands of yarn held together.

Afghan
With A, cast on 81 sts.

Row 1 (WS): K1, *[p2tog, (k1, p1, k1) in next st] 3 times, k1, [(k1, p1, k1) in next st, p2tog] 3 times, k1; rep from * 3 times—105 sts.

Row 2: K1, *p2tog, p9, (inc) twice, p10, p2tog, p1; rep from * twice, p2tog, p9, (inc) twice, p10, p2tog, k1.

Row 3: K1, *[p3tog, (k1, p1, k1) in next st] 3 times, k1, [(k1, p1, k1) in next st, p3tog] 3 times, k1; rep from * 3 times.

Row 4: Rep Row 2.

Rows 5–71: Rep Rows 3–4 in the following color sequence:

6 rows with 2 strands A.

2 rows with 1 strand each C and D.

10 rows with 2 strands B.

2 rows with 1 strand each C and D.

10 rows with 2 strands A.

2 rows with 1 strand each C and D.

10 rows with 2 strands B.

2 rows with 1 strand each C and D.

10 rows with 2 strands A.

2 rows with 1 strand each C and D.

11 rows with 2 strands B.

Bind off as follows: With B, k1 *[p2tog] twice, p1, p2tog, p10, p2tog, p2, [p2tog] twice, p1; rep from * twice, [p2tog] twice, p1, p2tog, p10, p2tog, p2, [p2tog] twice, k1. ●

Baby Love

If it's something for baby that you seek, you've come to the right place.

You'll find the cutest creations to wrap the new arrival in. All projects are

featured in the softest fibers made especially for little ones.

Crested Baby Blanket

Experienced knitters will enjoy creating this crested pattern in a chunky-weight yarn.

Design by Thanh Nguyen, courtesy of Premier Yarns

Skill Level
■■■■ EXPERIENCED

Finished Size
Approx 35 x 33 inches

Materials
- Premier Yarns/Deborah Norville Collection Serenity Chunky Weight (bulky; 100% acrylic; 109 yds/3½ oz per ball): 6 balls golden #DN500-03
- Size 11 (8mm) 32-inch circular needle

Gauge
25 sts and 35 rows (1 pat rep) = 7½ inches/19cm.

To save time, take time to check gauge.

Special Abbreviations
Make 1 purlwise (M1pwise): Insert LH needle from back to front under strand running between sts, p1.

Lifted Increase-Right purl (LI-Rp): Insert RH needle into right leg of st just below next st; place it onto LH needle and purl it.

Lifted Increase-Left purl (LI-Lp): Insert LH needle from back to front into left leg of st 2 rows below last completed st; p1-tbl.

Wrap and Turn (W/T): Bring yarn to RS of work between needles, slip next st pwise to RH needle, bring yarn around this st to WS, slip st back to LH needle, turn work to beg working back in other direction.

Pattern Stitches
Trough (multiple of 24 sts + 3)
Row 1 (WS): Sl 1, purl to last st, k1.
Row 2 (RS): Sl 1, knit to end.
Row 3: Sl 1, p1, *p2, [k4, p1] 3 times, k4, p3; rep from * to last st, k1.

Row 4: Sl 1, *k1, [M1pwise, k1] twice, [ssp, p2, k1] twice, [p2, p2tog, k1] twice, M1pwise, k1, M1pwise; rep from * to last st, k2.
Row 5: Sl 1, p1, *[k1, p1] twice, [k3, p1] 4 times, [k1, p1] twice; rep from * to last st, k1.
Row 6: Sl 1, *[k1, p1, LI-Rp] twice, [k1, ssp, p1] twice, [k1, p1, p2tog] twice, [k1, LI-Lp, p1] twice; rep from * to last 2 sts, k2.
Row 7: Sl 1, p1, *k2, p1; rep from * to last st, k1.
Row 8: Sl 1, *[k1, p2, LI-Rp] twice, [k1, ssp] twice, [k1, p2tog] twice, [k1, LI-Lp, p2] twice; rep from * to last 2 sts, k2.
Row 9: Sl 1, p1, *[k3, p1] twice, [k1, p1] 4 times, [k3, p1] 4 times; rep from * to last st, k1.
Row 10: Sl 1, *[k1, p3, LI-Rp] twice, [ssk] twice, k1, [k2tog] twice, LI-Lp, p3, k1, LI-Lp, p3; rep from * to last 2 sts, k2, k2.
Rep Rows 1–10 for pat.

Crest (multiple of 24 sts + 3)
Row 1 (WS): Sl 1, purl to last st, k1.
Row 2 (RS): Sl 1, knit to end.
Row 3: Sl 1, p1, *k4, p1, k4, p5, [k4, p1] twice; rep from * to last st, k1.
Row 4: Sl 1,*[k1, p2, p2tog] twice, [k1, M1pwise] 4 times, [k1, ssp, p2] twice; rep from * to last 2 sts, k2.
Row 5: Sl 1, p1, *[k3, p1] twice, [k1, p1] 4 times, [k3, p1] twice; rep from * to last st, k1.
Row 6: Sl 1, *[k1, p1, p2tog] twice, [k1, LI-Lp, p1] twice, [k1, p1, LI-Rp] twice, [k1, ssp, p1] twice; rep from * to last 2 sts, k2.
Row 7: Sl 1, p1, *k2, p1; rep from * to last st, k1.
Row 8: Sl 1, *[k1, p2tog] twice, [k1, LI-Lp, p2] twice, [k1, p2, LI-Rp] twice, [k1, ssp] twice; rep from * to last 2 sts, k2.
Row 9: Sl 1, p1, *[k1, p1] twice, [k3, p1] 4 times, [k1, p1] twice; rep from * to last st, k1.
Row 10: Sl 1, *k1, [k2tog] twice, [LI-Lp, p3, k1] twice, p3, LI-R, k1, p3, LI-Rp, [ssk] twice; rep from * to last 2 sts, k2.
Rep Rows 1–10 for pat.

Pattern Notes

Circular needle is used to accommodate large number of stitches; do not join, work back and forth in rows.

A chart is provided for those preferring to work from a chart.

Blanket

Cast on 99 sts.

Rows 1–60: [Work Rows 1–10 of Trough pat] 6 times.

Rows 61–122: [Work Rows 1–10 of Crest pat] 6 times, then rep Rows 1 and 2 once more.

Bind off all sts.

Side Borders

With RS facing, pick up and knit 99 sts evenly along left edge of blanket.

Work in Crest pat in short rows as follows:

Row 1 (WS): Work Crest pat Row 1.

Rows 2 and 3: Work Crest pat Rows 2 and 3 to last 2 sts, W/T.

Rows 4 and 5: Work established pat to last 3 sts, W/T.

Rows 6 and 7: Work established pat to last 4 sts, W/T.

Rows 8 and 9: Work established pat to last 5 sts, W/T.

Rows 10 and 11: Work established pat to last 6 sts, W/T.

Row 12: Work pat Row 2, working each wrap tog with wrapped st.

Bind off all sts, working each wrap tog with wrapped st.

Work 2nd border in same manner.

Finishing

Weave in all ends. Block to finished measurements. ●

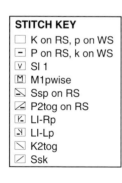

STITCH KEY
- ☐ K on RS, p on WS
- ⊟ P on RS, k on WS
- Ⅴ Sl 1
- Ⓜ M1pwise
- ◢ Ssp on RS
- ◿ P2tog on RS
- Ⓚ LI-Rp
- ⬊ LI-Lp
- ◣ K2tog
- ◹ Ssk

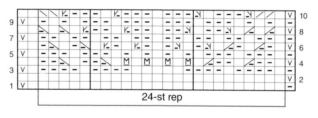

24-st rep

CREST CHART

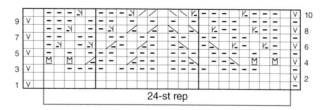

24-st rep

TROUGH CHART

Heaven-Sent Baby Blanket

Knit a soft ribbed blankie for a baby you love—so perfect in any color combination, you might want to make more than one!

Design by Veronica Manno, courtesy of Red Heart

. . . .

Skill Level
◖□□□ BEGINNER

Finished Size
36 inches wide x 32 inches long

Materials
- Red Heart Moon & Stars (worsted weight; 52% acrylic/48% nylon; 110 yds/50g per ball): 4 balls each blue eyes #3835 (A) and snow #3001 (B)
- Size 8 (5mm) 29-inch circular needle or size needed to obtain gauge

Gauge
16 sts and 22 rows = 4 inches/10cm in St st.

To save time, take time to check gauge.

Pattern Note
Circular needle is used to accommodate large number of stitches; do not join, work back and forth in rows.

Blanket
With A, cast on 168 sts.

Rows 1–6: With A,*k6, p6; rep from * to end.

Rows 7–12: With B, rep Rows 1–6.

Rep Rows 1–12 until piece measures 36 inches, ending with a Row 6 or 12.

Bind off.

Finishing
Weave in ends. Block to finished measurements. ●

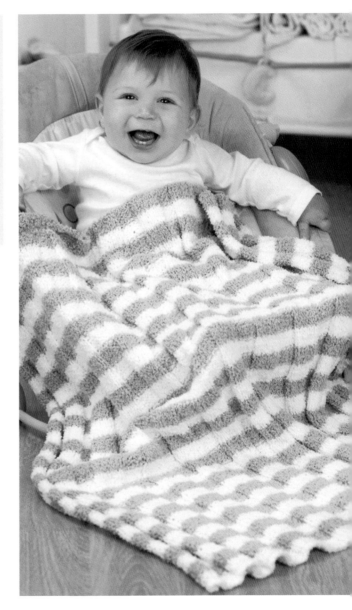

Candy Stripes Blankie

The perfect gift to make while you're waiting for baby to arrive, this blankie is easy to knit in pretty pastels that are perfect for a boy or a girl.

Design by Kathy Sasser

Skill Level
■■□□ EASY

Finished Size
Approx 30 x 40 (36 x 44) inches

Materials
• Bernat Cottontots (worsted weight; 100% cotton; 150 yds/85g per ball): 7 (9) balls sweet dreams ombré #91231
• Size 7 (4.5mm) 32-inch circular needle or size needed to obtain gauge
• Tapestry needle
• Stitch markers

4 MEDIUM

Gauge
Approx 18 sts = 4 inches/10cm in pat.

To save time, take time to check gauge.

Pattern Stitches
Modified Farrow Rib (multiple of 4 sts)
Row 1: *K3, p1; rep from * across.
Rep Row 1 for pat.

Moss St (multiple of 2 sts)
Row 1 (RS): *K1, p1; rep from * across.
Row 2: *P1, k1; rep from * across.
Rep Rows 1 and 2 for pat.

Pattern Note
Circular needle is used to accommodate large number of stitches; do not join, work back and forth in rows.

Afghan
Cast on 136 (164) sts.

Work [Rows 1 and 2 of Moss St pat] 5 (7) times.

Work 6 (10) sts in established Moss St pat, place marker, work Modified Farrow Rib pat over next 124 (144) sts, place marker, work 6 (10) sts in established Moss St pat.

Continue in pats as established, working first and last 6 (10) sts in Moss St pat and sts between markers in Modified Farrow Rib pat until piece measures approximately 38½ (42) inches from beg.

Work in 10 (14) rows in Moss St pat.

Bind off.

Weave in ends and block to measurements. ●

Huggable Hooded Blankie

Keep baby's head covered and warm with a hooded blankie knit in a soft, chunky-weight yarn.

Design by Scarlet Taylor

Skill Level

■■□□□ EASY

Finished Size
Approx 30 inches square (before folding and excluding tassels)

Materials
• Plymouth Yarn Co. Oh My! (bulky weight; 100% nylon; 70 yds/ 50g per ball): 14 balls soft lime #19
• Size 10 (6mm) needles or size needed to obtain gauge
• Stitch marker
• 6-inch-wide cardboard piece

Gauge
Gauge not critical to project.

Special Abbreviation
Reverse yarn over (reverse yo): Wrap yarn in reverse of a typical yo so that no hole is made. In other words, bring yarn forward to RS over RH needle, and then take it back between needles to WS into knit position. Be sure to knit yo through front loop on following row.

Blanket
Cast on 4 sts. Knit 2 rows even.

Inc row: K1, reverse yo, knit to last st, end reverse yo, k1—6 sts.

Place a marker to designate this row as inc row.

Continue to work in garter st, rep inc row [every other row] 82 times—170 sts.

Knit 1 row even.

Dec row: K1, ssk, knit to last 3 sts, k2tog, k1—168 sts.

Continue to work in garter st, rep dec row [every other row] 82 times—4 sts.

Work 3 rows even on rem 4 sts.

Hood
Inc row: K1, reverse yo, knit to last st, end reverse yo, k1—6 sts.

Continue to work in garter st, rep inc row [every other row] 40 times—86 sts.

Bind off all sts.

Assembly
Referring to Figure 1, fold hood down 10 inches and sew edges to corner edges of blanket.

Make 4 tassels by wrapping yarn 32 times around a 6-inch-wide piece of cardboard. With separate 6-inch strand, tie tog at top, slip off cardboard and wrap another strand approx 1 inch below top, hiding ends in tassel. Cut strands at bottom, trim even and attach 1 tassel securely to each corner of blanket. ●

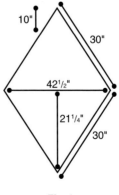

Fig. 1

Chevron Fantastic Afghan

Each of these six chevron patterns uses a different combination of double increases and decreases. Color gradations are created by holding two strands of yarn together, adding further emphasis to the pattern sections.

Design by Beth Whiteside

Skill Level
■ ■ □ □ EASY

Finished Sizes
Approx 30 x 36 (45 x 56) inches Instructions are given for smaller size, with larger size in parentheses. When only 1 number is given, it applies to both sizes.

Materials
- Worsted weight yarn (225 yds/100g per ball): 2 (3) balls dark blue (A), 2 (4) balls medium blue (B), 2 (4) balls light blue (C), 1 (3) ball(s) white/blue tweed (D)
- Size 15 (10mm) 24-inch (36-inch) circular needle or size needed to obtain gauge

Gauge
11½ sts and 15 rows = 4 inches/10cm in Chevron pat with 2 strands of yarn held tog.

Note: Measure straight across pat vertically and horizontally (not in direction of sts).

To save time, take time to check gauge.

Special Abbreviations
Knit in front and back (kf&b)): Knit into front and back of next st.

Knit, yarn over, Knit (KOK): [K1, yo, k1] in next st.

Make 1 Left (M1L): Inc 1 by inserting LH needle from front to back under strand between st just worked and next st, k1-tbl.

Make 1 Right (M1R): Inc 1 by inserting LH needle from back to front under strand between last st worked and next st, knit st.

Central Double Decrease (CDD): Sl next 2 sts as if to k2tog, k1, p2sso.

Knit 3 together (k3tog): Knit 3 tog.

Slip, slip, slip, knit (sssk): Slip next 3 sts one at a time kwise, k3tog-tbl.

Pattern Notes
Yarn is held double throughout; when there is only 1 ball, find the inner and outer ends and hold them together as 1.

Circular needle is used to accommodate large number of stitches; do not join, work back and forth in rows.

Note that 1 stitch is added in Chevron Pat 3 and decreased at the end of Chevron Pat 6.

Afghan
Holding 2 strands of A tog, cast on 85 (129) sts. Knit 6 rows.

Cut 1 strand of A, join 1 strand of B.

Chevron Pat 1
Rows 1, 3 and 5 (RS): K4, *k2tog, k2, [kf&b] twice, k3, ssk; rep from * to last 4 sts, end k4.

Rows 2, 4 and 6: K4, purl to last 4 sts, end k4.

Cut A, join 2nd strand of B.

Row 7: K4, *k2tog, k2, [kf&b] twice, k3, ssk; rep from * to last 4 sts, end k4.

Rows 8–12: Knit across.

Cut 1 strand of B; join 1 strand of C.

Chevron Pat 2
Rows 13, 15 and 17 (RS): K4, *k2tog, k3, KOK, k3, ssk; rep from * to last 4 sts, end k4.

Rows 14, 16 and 18: K4, purl to last 4 sts, end k4.

Cut B, join 2nd strand of C.

Row 19: K4, *k2tog, k3, KOK, k3, ssk; rep from * to last 4 sts, end k4.

Rows 20–24: Knit across.

Cut 1 strand of C; join 1 strand of D.

Chevron Pat 3

Note: 1 st is added in first row.

Row 25 (RS): K4, k2tog, k3, yo, k2, yo, k3, *sk2p, k3, yo, k2, yo, k3; rep from * to last 5 sts, k5—86 (130) sts.

Rows 27 and 29: K4, k2tog, k3, yo, k2, yo, k3, *sk2p, k3, yo, k2, yo, k3; rep from * to last 6 sts, end ssk, k4.

Rows 26, 28 and 30: K4, purl to last 4 sts, end k4.

Cut C, join 2nd strand of D.

Row 31: K4, k2tog, k3, yo, k2, yo, k3, *sk2p, k3, yo, k2, yo, k3; rep from * to last 6 sts, end ssk, k4.

Rows 32–36: Knit across.

Cut 1 strand of D; join 1 strand of C.

Chevron Pat 4

Rows 37, 39 and 41 (RS): K4, k2tog, k3, M1L, k2, M1R, k3, *k3tog, k3, M1L, k2, M1R, k3; rep from * to last 6 sts, end ssk, k4.

Rows 38, 40 and 42: K4, purl to last 4 sts, end k4.

Cut D, join 2nd strand of C.

Row 43: K4, k2tog, k3, M1L, k2, M1R, k3, *k3tog, k3, M1L, k2, M1R, k3; rep from * to last 6 sts, end ssk, k4.

Rows 44–48: Knit across.

Cut 1 strand of C; join 1 strand of B.

Chevron Pat 5

Rows 49, 51 and 53 (RS): K4, k2tog, k3, yo, k2, yo, k3, *sssk, k3, yo, k2, yo, k3; rep from * to last 6 sts, end ssk, k4.

Rows 50, 52 and 54: K4, purl to last 4 sts, end k4.

Cut C, join 2nd strand of B.

Row 55: K4, k2tog, k3, yo, k2, yo, k3, *sssk, k3, yo, k2, yo, k3; rep from * to last 6 sts, end ssk, k4.

Rows 56–60: Knit.

Cut 1 strand of B; join 1 strand of A.

Chevron Pat 6

Note: 1 st dec in last row.

Rows 61, 63 and 65 (RS): K4, k2tog, k3, M1L, k2, M1R, k3, *CDD, k3, M1L, k2, M1R, k3; rep from * to last 6 sts, end ssk, k4.

Rows 62, 64 and 66: K4, purl to last 4 sts, end k4.

Cut B, join 2nd strand of A.

Row 67: K4, k2tog, k3, M1L, k2, M1R, k3, *CDD, k3, M1L, k2, M1R, k3; rep from * to last 6 sts, end ssk, k4.

Rows 68–71: Knit across.

Row 72: K4, k2tog, knit to end—85 (129) sts.

[Rep 6 Chevron pats 1–6] 1 (2) more time(s). Knit 1 row.

Bind off all sts. ●

Patchwork Checks

Intarsia bows or chicks combined with checks are fun to stitch while waiting for your bundle of joy.

Design by Scarlet Taylor

Finished Size
Approx 30 x 30 inches

Girl's Afghan

Materials
- Bernat Softee Baby (DK weight; 100% acrylic; 395 yds/5 oz per ball): 1 ball each white #02000 (A), pink #02001 (B), 2 balls prettiest pink #30205 (C)
- Size 6 (4mm) straight and 24-inch circular needles or size needed to obtain gauge
- Size 7 (4.5mm) needles or size needed to obtain gauge
- Stitch markers

Boy's Afghan

Materials
- Bernat Softee Baby (DK weight; 100% acrylic; 395 yds/5 oz per ball): 1 ball each white #02000 (A), pale blue #02002 (B), lemon #02003 (D)
- Bernat Satin Sport (light weight; 100% acrylic; 237 yds/85g per ball): 4 balls clear sky #03141 (C)
- Size 6 (4mm) straight and 24-inch circular needles or size needed to obtain gauge
- Size 7 (4.5mm) needles or size needed to obtain gauge
- Small amount black embroidery floss or yarn
- Stitch markers

Gauge

Gingham square: 28 sts and 30 rows = 5 inches/12.5cm square with larger needles.

Solid square: 28 sts and 38 rows = 5 inches/12.5cm square with smaller needles in St st.

Bow or chick square: 27 sts and 38 rows = 5 inches/12.5cm square with smaller needles in St st.

To save time, take time to check gauge.

Girl's Afghan

Pattern Note
When working gingham square, carry color not in use loosely across back.

Gingham Square
Make 12

With larger needles and C, cast on 28 sts.

Row 1 (RS): K3 B, *k2 C, k2 B; rep from * to last st, k1 B.

Row 2: P3 B, *p2 C, p2 B; rep from * to last st, p1 B.

Row 3: K3 A, *k2 B, k2 A; rep from * to last st, k1 A.

Row 4: P3 A, *p2 B, p2 A; rep from * to last st, p1 A.

Rows 5–28: [Rep Rows 1–4] 6 times.

Rows 29 and 30: Rep Rows 1 and 2.

Bind off all sts with C.

Solid Square
Make 12

With smaller needles and C, cast on 28 sts.
Work in St st until block measures 5 inches, ending with a WS row.

Bind off all sts.

Bow Square
Make 12

With smaller needles and A, cast on 27 sts.

Rows 1 and 2: Beg with a RS row, work 2 rows in St st.

Row 3 (RS): Join C, k1 C, *k1 A, k1 C; rep from * across.

Row 4: P1 A, *p1 C, p1 A; rep from * across. Cut C.

Rows 5–14: With A, work 10 rows in St st.

Row 15 (RS): K9, place marker, work Row 1 of Bow Chart on page 85 over next 9 sts, place marker, work to end.

Rows 16–24: Continue as established, working Rows 2–10 of chart pat between markers.

Rows 25–34: Removing markers, continue in St st and A only for 10 rows more.

Row 35 (RS): Join C, k1 C, *k1 A, k1 C; rep from * across.

Row 36: P1 A, *p1 C, p1 A; rep from * across. Cut C.

Rows 37 and 38: With A, and work 2 rows St st.

Bind off all sts.

Assembly
Referring to Assembly Diagram for placement of squares, sew 6 rows of 6 squares each tog.

Border
With smaller circular needle and A, pick up and knit 126 sts evenly across 1 edge of afghan. Do not join; work back and forth in garter st, inc 1 st at each end of needle every other row until border measures approx 1 inch. Bind off loosely.

Rep for rem 3 sides of afghan. Seam mitered corners.

Boy's Afghan

Gingham Square
Make 12 as for Girl's Afghan.

Solid Square
Make 12 as for Girl's Afghan.

Chick Square
Make 12

With smaller needles and B, cast on 27 sts. Beg with a RS row, work 14 rows in St st.

Next row (RS): Knit 8 sts, place marker, work Row 1 of Chick Chart over next 11 sts, place marker, work to end.

Continue as established, working pat from chart between markers until Row 10 has been completed.

Removing markers, continue in St st and B only for 14 rows more.

Bind off all sts.

Assembly
Work embroidery on chicks as shown on chart.

Referring to Assembly Diagram for placement of squares, sew 6 rows of 6 squares each tog.

Border
With smaller circular needle and C, RS facing, pick up and knit 142 sts along 1 edge of afghan. Do not join. Work in k2, p2 rib, inc 1 st at each side [every row] 8 times. Bind off in rib.

Rep for rem 3 sides of afghan. Seam mitered corners. •

CHICK CHART

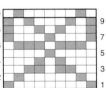

BOW CHART

COLOR KEY
- ☐ B
- ☐ D
- ✎ Straight st in black

COLOR KEY
- ☐ B
- ☐ D
- ✎ Straight st in black

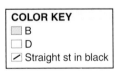

SQUARE KEY
- 1 Gingham
- 2 Solid
- 3 Chick or bow

1	2	3	1	2	3
2	3	1	2	3	1
3	1	2	3	1	2
1	2	3	1	2	3
2	3	1	2	3	1
3	1	2	3	1	2

ASSEMBLY DIAGRAM

3-D Baby Blanket

An old quilt design becomes a new knit baby blanket in bright, sunny colors.

Design by Kathy Wesley
Inspired by Kimberly Gallivan

Skill Level
■■■□ INTERMEDIATE

Finished Size
39 x 39 inches

Materials
- Plymouth Yarn Co. Encore DK (light weight; 75% acrylic/25% wool; 150 yds/50g per ball): 6 balls yellow #1382 (A) and 2 balls orange #1383 (B)
- Size 6 (4mm) 32-inch circular needle or size needed to obtain gauge

Gauge
22 sts and 28 rows = 4 inches/10cm in pat.

To save time, take time to check gauge.

Special Abbreviation
Centered Double Decrease (CDD): Sl next 2 sts as if to k2tog, k1, pass 2 slipped sts over knit st.

Pattern Note
Circular needle used to accommodate stitches; do not join, work back and forth in rows.

Blanket
With A, cast on 193 sts.

Row 1 (RS): K1, *yo, ssk, k7, k2tog, yo, k1; rep from * across.

Row 2: *P3, k7, p2; rep from * to last st, p1.

Row 3: K1, *yo, k1, ssk, k5, k2tog, k1, yo, k1; rep from * across.

Row 4: *P4, k5, p3; rep from * to last st, p1.

Row 5: K1, *yo, k2, ssk, k3, k2tog, k2, yo, k1; rep from * across.

Row 6: *P5, k3, p4; rep from * to last st, p1.

Row 7: K1, *yo, k3, ssk, k1, k2tog, k3, yo, k1; rep from * across.

Row 8: *K2, [p4, k1] twice; rep from * to last st, k1.

Row 9: K1, *k1, yo, k3, CDD, k3, yo, k2; rep from * across.

Row 10: *K3, p7, k2; rep from * to last st, k1.

Row 11: K1, *k2, yo, k2, CDD, k2, yo, k3; rep from * across.

Row 12: *K4, p5, k3; rep from * to last st, k1.

Row 13: K1, *k3, yo, k1, CDD, k1, yo, k4; rep from * across.

Row 14: *K5, p3, k4; rep from * to last st, k1.

Row 15: K1, *k4, yo, CDD, yo, k5; rep from * across.

Row 16: Rep Row 14.

Row 17: K1, *k3, k2tog, yo, k1, yo, ssk, k4; rep from * across.

Row 18: Rep Row 12.

Row 19: K1, *k2, k2tog, [k1, yo] twice, k1, ssk, k3; rep from * across.

Row 20: Rep Row 10.

Row 21: K1, *k1, k2tog, k2, yo, k1, yo, k2, ssk, k2; rep from * across.

Row 22: *K2, p9, k1; rep from * to last st, k1.

Row 23: K1, *k2tog, k3, yo, k1, yo, k3, ssk, k1; rep from * across.

Row 24: *K1, p4, k3, p4; rep from * to last st, k1.

Row 25: K1, k2tog, *k2, [yo, k3] twice, CDD, k1; rep from * to last 10 sts, k2, [yo, k3] twice, ssk.

Row 26: Rep Row 4.

Row 27: K1, k2tog, *k1, yo, k5, yo, k2, CDD, k1; rep from * to last 10 sts, k1, yo, k5, yo, k2, ssk.

Row 28: Rep Row 2.

Row 29: K1, k2tog, *yo, k7, yo, k1, CDD, k1; rep from * to last 10 sts, yo, k7, yo, k1, ssk.

Row 30: *P2, k9, p1; rep from * to last st, p1.

Row 31: K2tog, *yo, k9, yo, CDD; rep from * to last 11 sts, yo, k9, yo, ssk.

Row 32: Rep Row 30.

Rep [Rows 1–32] 8 times. Do not bind off.

Garter Border
With RS facing and B, knit across, dec 3 sts—190 sts.

Top border
Row 1 (WS): Knit across.

Row 2 (RS): K1, knit in front and back of next st, knit to last 2 sts, knit in front and back of next st, k1.

Rows 3–14: Rep [Rows 1 and 2] 6 times.

Bind off.

Bottom border
With RS facing and B, pick up and knit 190 sts across cast-on edge of blanket.

Rep Rows 1–14 of Top Border.

Bind off.

Side borders
With RS facing and B, pick up and knit 190 sts along 1 side edge, picking up at a rate of 3 sts for every 4 rows.

Rep Rows 1–14 of Top Border.

Bind off.

Rep along opposite side.

Sew corner seams. ●

Soft & Snuggly Baby Blanket

Work this baby blanket back and forth in rows to create this sweet, subtle pattern.

Design by Melissa Leapman

Finished Size
43 x 46 inches

Materials
- Red Heart Moon & Stars (worsted weight; 52% acrylic/48% nylon; 110 yds/50g per ball): 11 balls mint jelly #3668
- Size 9 (5.5mm) 29-inch circular needle or size needed to obtain gauge
- Size 10 (6mm) 29-inch circular needle

Gauge
16 sts and 22 rows = 4 inches/10cm in St st with smaller needle.

To save time, take time to check gauge.

Special Abbreviation
Make 1 (M1): Insert LH needle from front to back under the running thread between the last st worked and next st on RH needle; knit (or purl) into the back of resulting loop.

Pattern Stitch
Lace (multiple of 10 sts + 15)
Row 1 (RS): K10, *k2tog, yo, k8; rep from * to last 5 sts, k2tog, yo, k3.
Row 2 and all WS rows: Purl.
Row 3: K9, *k2tog, yo, k8; rep from * to last 6 sts, k2tog, yo, k4.
Row 5: K8, *k2tog, yo, k8; rep from * to last 7 sts, k2tog, yo, k5.
Row 7: K7, *k2tog, yo, k8; rep from * to last 8 sts, k2tog, yo, k6.
Row 9: K2, *yo, ssk, k2, k2tog, yo, k4; rep from * to last 3 sts, k3.

Row 11: K3, *yo, ssk, k8; rep from * to last 2 sts, k2.
Row 13: K4, *yo, ssk, k8; rep from * to last st, k1.
Row 15: K5, *yo, ssk, k8; rep from * to end.
Row 17: K6, *yo, ssk, k8; rep from * to last 9 sts, yo, ssk, k7.
Row 19: K7, *yo, ssk, k2, k2tog, yo, k4; rep from * to last 8 sts, yo, ssk, k2, k2tog, yo, k2.
Row 20: Rep Row 2.
Rep Rows 1–20

Pattern Notes
Blanket is worked back and forth in rows; a circular needle is used to accommodate the large number of sts.

A chart is provided for those preferring to work from a chart.

Blanket
With smaller needle, cast on 155 sts.

Work Lace pat until piece measures 42 inches, ending with Row 8 or 18.

Bind off.

Top & Bottom Border
With RS facing and larger needle, pick up and knit 155 sts along cast-on or bound-off row.

Row 1 (WS): P2, *k1, p1; rep from * to last st, p1.

Row 2: K2, M1 kwise, work in established rib to last 2 sts, M1 kwise, k2.

Row 3: P3, *k1, p1; rep from * to last 4 sts, k1, p3.

Row 4: K2, M1 pwise, *k1, p1; rep from * to last 3 sts, k1, M1 pwise, k2.

Rep Rows 1–4 once more, then Row 1 once.

Bind off.

Rep along opposite edge.

Side Border
With RS facing and larger needle, pick up and knit 167 sts along side edge.

Work as for top and bottom border.

Finishing
Sew mitered corners of border tog. Weave in ends. Block to finished measurements. ●

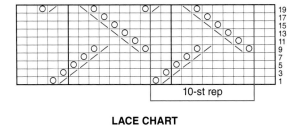

LACE CHART

	STITCH KEY
□	K on RS, p on WS
⊙	Yo
◣	Ssk
◢	K2tog

Note: *Only RS rows are shown; purl across all WS rows.*

Rainbow Car Seat Blanket

Bright, multi-hued yarn looks especially cheerful as a cute, car seat blanket to keep baby warm and snuggly.

Design by Kennita Tully

. . . .

Skill Level

⬤⬤⬤▢ INTERMEDIATE

Finished Sizes
Blanket: Approx 36 inches square
Car-seat cover-up: Approx 24 inches square

Materials
- Plymouth Yarn Co. Dreambaby DK (light weight; 50% microfiber acrylic/50% nylon 183 yds/50g per ball): 11 balls bright multi #210 for blanket; 5 balls bright multi #210 for car-seat cover-up
- Size 6 (4mm) 36–40 inch circular needle or size needed to obtain gauge
- Tapestry needlee

Gauge
17 sts and 39 rows = 4 inches/10cm in pat st.

To save time, take time to check gauge.

Pattern Stitch
Reversible St (worked over an odd number of sts)

Note: Sts inc on Row 1 and dec back to original st count on Row 3.

Row 1: K2, *yo, k1; rep from * to last st, end p1.
Row 2: K1, purl across.
Rows 3: K2, [k2tog] to last st, end p1.
Rows 4 and 5: K2, *yo, k2tog; rep from * to last st, end p1.
Rows 6 and 7: Knit to last st, p1.
Rep Rows 1–7 for pat.

Pattern Notes
Instructions are given for car-seat cover-up with changes for larger blanket in parentheses.

This pattern is reversible, so no right or wrong side is indicated.

Blanket
Cast on 101 (153) sts.

Knit 2 rows.

Beg with Row 1, work Reversible St pat until piece measures approx 24 (36) inches or desired length ending with Row 7.

Bind off all sts.

Finishing
Weave in all ends. Wash and pin to measurements. ●

Ruffled Blocks Baby Blanket

A beautifully ruffled edge, worked and then sewn on, gives this exquisite blanket an heirloom quality.

Design by Dawn Brocco

Skill Level
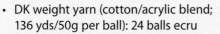 INTERMEDIATE

Finished Size
Approx 38 x 49 inches (including ruffled edge)

Materials

- DK weight yarn (cotton/acrylic blend; 136 yds/50g per ball): 24 balls ecru
- Size 8 (5mm) 24- or 29-inch circular needles and 2 double-point needles or size needed to obtain gauge
- Cable needle
- Stitch holder
- Tapestry needle

Gauge
16 sts and 24 rows = 4 inches/10cm in St st, using 2 strands of yarn.

To save time, take time to check gauge.

Special Abbreviations
Crossed Twist (CT): Slip next 3 sts to cn and hold in back, knit next st, sl 2 sts from cn to LH needle, bring cn with rem st to front, k2 from LH needle, knit st from cn.

Wrap/Turn (W/T): Slip next st from left to right needle, bring yarn to front between needles, return slipped st to LH needle, turn work.

Pattern Stitches
Crossed-St Block
Row 1 (RS): Knit.
Row 2: *K2, p6; rep from * across to last 2 sts, k2.
Rows 3–8: Rep [Rows 1 and 2] 3 times.
Row 9: K7, *sl 1p, k2, sl 1p, k4; rep from * across to last 3 sts, k3.
Row 10: K7, *sl 1p wyif, k2, sl 1p wyif, k4; rep from * across to last 3 sts, k3.
Rows 11 and 12: Rep Rows 9 and 10.

Row 13: K7, *CT, k4; rep from * across to last 3 sts, k3.
Row 14: Rep Row 2.
Rep Rows 1–14 for pat.

Welted Ruffle
Note: W/T is used to work short rows on Rows 2 and 5.
Row 1: Knit.
Row 2: P10, W/T, k10.
Row 3: P10, k3.
Row 4: K3, p10.
Row 5: K10, W/T, p10.
Row 6: Knit.
Rep Rows 1–6 for pat.

Pattern Notes
Blanket is worked using 2 strands of yarn held together throughout.

Ruffled edge is worked separately, and then sewn on blanket.

Circular needle used to accommodate stitches; do not join, work back and forth in rows.

Blanket
With 2 strands of yarn, cast on 130 sts.

Work [Rows 1–14 of Crossed-St Block pat] 18 times.

Rep Rows 1–8.

Bind off as to knit.

Ruffle Edging
Cast on 13 sts. Work Welted Ruffle pat back and forth on dpns until 219 ruffles (438 garter rows on welt or short edge) are completed, do not bind off, sl sts to a holder.

Finishing
Lay blanket flat with RS facing. Using 1 strand of yarn and tapestry needle, beg at upper LH corner of long edge of blanket, attach ruffle edging to blanket using overcast st, matching garter ridges of blanket to garter ridges of welt on ruffle edging. At each

corner, ease 2 or 3 garter welt ridges around edge to relieve puckering.

On short sides of the blanket, before sewing tog, pin 4 welt garter ridges to each 6 sts of blanket pat.

As you come to starting point, knit additional reps of welt pat, if necessary. Bind off pwise.

Sew ends of ruffle edging tog. Weave in all ends. •

Cozy Cable Afghan

With garter stitching and cable patterning, this afghan makes an impressive and thoughtful gift.

Design by Scarlet Taylor

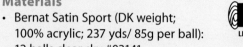

Skill Level

◼◼◼◻ INTERMEDIATE

Finished Size

Approx 32 x 38½ inches

Materials

- Bernat Satin Sport (DK weight; 100% acrylic; 237 yds/ 85g per ball): 12 balls clear sky #03141
- Size 10 (6mm) 29-inch circular knitting needle or size needed to obtain gauge
- Cable needle
- Crochet hook
- Stitch markers

3 LIGHT

Gauge

18 sts and 24 rows = 4 inches/10cm with 2 strands of yarn in Garter Ridge pat.

To save time, take time to check gauge.

Special Abbreviations

Cable Back (CB): Sl next 2 sts to cn and hold in back of work, k2, k2 from cn.

Cable Front (CF): Sl next 2 sts to cn and hold in front of work, k2, k2 from cn.

Back Cross (BC): Sl next st to cn and hold in back of work, k2, p1 st from cn.

Front Cross (FC): Sl next 2 sts to cn and hold in front of work, p1, k2 sts from cn.

Pattern Stitches

Garter Ridge (multiple of 10 sts + 4)
Row 1 (RS): P4, *k6, p4; rep from * across.
Row 2: K4, *p6, k4; rep from * across.
Row 3: Purl across.
Row 4: Knit across.
Rep Rows 1–4 for pat.

Border (worked over 6 sts)
Row 1 (RS): Knit.
Row 2: Purl.
Row 3: Purl.
Row 4: Knit.

Cable (worked over 8 sts)
Row 1 (RS): K1, p1, k4, p1, k1.
Row 2: P1, k1, p4, k1, p1.
Row 3: K1, p1, CB, p1, k1.
Row 4: Rep Row 2.
Rep Rows 1–4 for pat.

Diamond Cable (worked over 14 sts)
Row 1 (RS): P1, k2, p8, k2, p1.
Row 2: K1, p2, k8, p2, k1.
Row 3 (RS): P1, FC, p6, BC, p1.
Row 4: K2, p2, k6, p2, k2.
Row 5: P2, FC, p4, BC, p2.
Row 6: K3, p2, k4, p2, k3.
Row 7: P3, FC, p2, BC, p3.
Row 8: K4, p2, k2, p2, k4.
Row 9: P4, FC, BC, p4.
Row 10: K5, p4, k5.
Row 11: P5, CF, p5.
Row 12: Rep Row 10.
Row 13: P5, k4, p5.
Row 14: Rep Row 10.
Row 15: Rep Row 11.
Row 16: Rep Row 10.
Row 17: P4, BC, FC, p4.
Row 18: K4, p2, k2, p2, k4.
Row 19: P3, BC, p2, FC, p3.
Row 20: K3, p2, k4, p2, k3.
Row 21: P2, BC, p4, FC, p2.
Row 22: K2, p2, k6, p2, k2.
Row 23: P1, BC, p6, FC, p1.
Row 24: K1, p2, k8, p2, k1.
Rep Rows 3–24 for pat.

Pattern Notes

Circular needle used to accommodate stitches; do not join, work back and forth in rows.

Use 2 strands of yarn held together throughout.

Markers are used between patterns for ease in identifying stitch patterns while working afghan.

Afghan

With 2 strands of yarn, cast on 154 sts.

Set-up pat

Work Row 1 of Border pat over first 6 sts, place marker, work Row 1 of Garter Ridge pat over next 24 sts, place marker, work Row 1 of Cable pat over next 8 sts, place marker, work Row 1 of Diamond Cable pat over next 14 sts, place marker, work Row 1 of Cable pat over next 8 sts, place marker, work Row 1 of Garter Ridge pat over next 34 sts, place marker, work Row 1 of Cable pat over next 8 sts, place marker, work Row 1 of Diamond Cable pat over next 14 sts, place marker, work Row 1 of Cable pat over next 8 sts, place marker, work Row 1 of Garter Ridge pat over next 24 sts, work Row 1 of Border pat over last 6 sts.

Continue in pats as established between markers, working until piece measures approx 38½ inches from beg, ending with a Row 24 of Diamond Cable pat.

Bind off loosely and weave in all ends.

Fringe

Cut 10-inch lengths of yarn. For each knot, fold 6 strands of yarn in half, insert crochet hook from back to front through st, pull folded strands through to back. Pull ends through fold and pull tightly.

Fringe each short end, placing knots evenly spaced across (about every 5th st). Trim ends even. ●

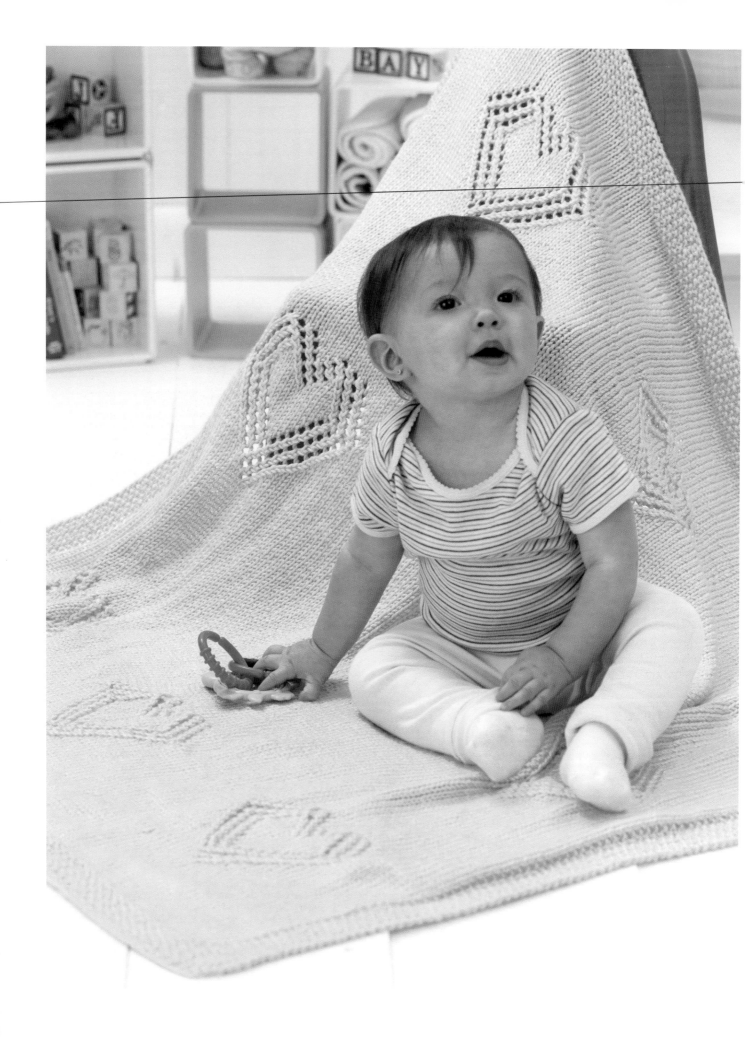

Sweet Hearts Baby Blanket

Make your little sweetheart a heart-filled blanket that shows her just how much you love her.

Design by Scarlet Taylor courtesy of Red Heart

· ·

Skill Level

■ ■ ■ ▢ INTERMEDIATE

Finished Size
36 x 36 inches

Materials
- Red Heart Soft Yarn (worsted weight; 100% acrylic; 256 yds/5 oz per skein): 4 skeins pink #6768
- Size 8 (5mm) 29-inch circular needle or size needed to obtain gauge
- 8 stitch markers in 2 colors

Gauge
18 sts and 24 rows = 4 inches/10cm in St st; 25 sts = 6 inches and 35 rows = 5 inches/12.5cm in Heart Motif.

To save time, take time to check gauge.

Pattern Stitches
Seed St (odd number of sts)
Row 1: K1, *p1, k1; rep from * across.
Rep Row 1 for pat.

Heart Motif (25 sts)
See Chart.

Pattern Note
A circular needle is used to accommodate the large number of stitches; do not join, work back and forth in rows.

Blanket
Cast on 161 sts.

Border
Work in Seed St pat until piece measures 1½ inches, ending with a WS row.

Body
Row 1 (RS): Work 7 sts in seed st, place border marker, knit to last 7 sts, place border marker, work seed st to end.

Maintaining first and last 7 sts in seed st for side borders, work even in St st until piece measures 4½ inches, ending with a WS row and on last row, dec 4 sts evenly across between markers—157 sts.

***Set-up row (RS):** Work 7 sts in seed st, k11, place marker, [work Row 1 of Heart Motif over next 25 sts, place marker, k23, place marker] twice, work Row 1 of Heart Motif over next 25 sts, place marker, k11, work 7 sts in seed st.

Maintaining border as established and St st between Heart Motifs, work until Row 35 of chart has been completed.

Next row (WS): Removing all but border markers, maintain border seed st and purl between markers.**

Maintaining border and working St st between markers, work even for 6 inches, ending with a WS row.***

Rep from * to *** once, then rep from * to **, inc 4 sts evenly across last row between markers—161 sts.

Maintaining border and working St st between markers, work even for 3 inches, ending with a WS row.

Border
Removing markers on first row, work in Seed St pat for 1½ inches.

Finishing
Weave in ends. ●

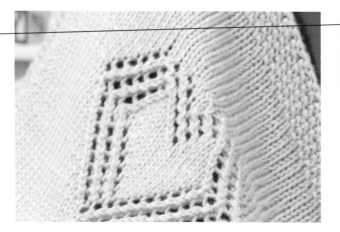

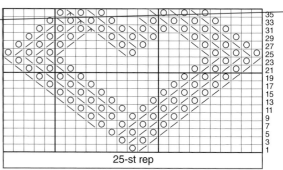

HEART CHART

Note: *Only RS rows are shown; purl across all WS rows.*

25-st rep

STITCH KEY
- ☐ K on RS, p on WS
- ⊙ Yo
- ◲ Ssk
- ◱ K2tog
- ⊼ Sk2p

Tempting Textures

If you're in the mood for creating richly-textured accents, the projects

that follow will provide you with unlimited possibilities.

Romantic Lace Afghan

Bobbles and lace combine to make this lovely afghan.

Design by Melissa Leapman

. . . .

Skill Level
■■■□ INTERMEDIATE

Finished Size
Approx 51 x 62 inches

Materials

- Lion Brand Wool-Ease (worsted weight; 86% acrylic/10% wool/4% rayon; 197 yds/85g per ball): 14 balls wheat #402
- Size 6 (4mm) circular needle
- Size 8 (5mm) circular needle or size needed to obtain gauge
- Tapestry needle

Gauge
18 sts and 22 rows = 4 inches/10cm with larger needles in pat.

To save time, take time to check gauge.

Pattern Notes
Circular needles are used to accommodate the large number of stitches; do not join, work back and forth in rows.

When working Row 1 of chart on first repeat, work stitch shown as bobble as a knit stitch; on subsequent repeats, work it as a bobble.

Special Abbreviation
Bobble: Knit into (front, back, front, back, front) of next st, turn; p5, turn; k5, turn; p2tog, p1, p2tog, turn; slip next 2 sts kwise, knit next st, p2sso.

Afghan
With smaller needle, use knit-on cast-on technique, cast on 225 sts.

Work 14 rows of garter st.

Change to larger needle and beg pat from Chart A, keeping 7 sts at each edge in garter st throughout. Rep Rows 1–20 until afghan measures approx 60 inches from beg, ending with Row 20 of chart.

Change to smaller needle and work 14 rows of garter st. Bind off all sts. Weave in ends. ●

STITCH KEY
- ☐ Knit on RS, purl on WS
- – Purl on RS, knit on WS
- ○ Yo
- ⟋ K2tog
- ⟍ Ssk
- ⟑ Sl next 2 sts at once as k2tog; knit next to st; p2sso
- ● Bobble

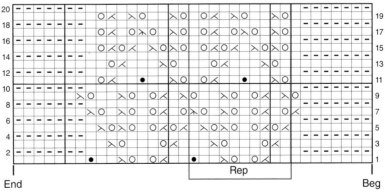

CHART A

Note: On Row 1 of chart, work the bobble as a plain knit st the first time; on subsequent reps, work it as a bobble.

Eyelet & Wavy-Cables Blanket

The pattern is attractive on both sides of this blanket and is suitable for either a lapghan or baby blanket.

Design by Suzanne Atkinson

Skill Level
 INTERMEDIATE

Finished Size
Approx 36 x 40 inches (after blocking)

Materials
• Worsted weight yarn (210 yds/ 100g per ball): 6 balls blue
• Size 8 (5mm) 29-inch circular needle or size needed to obtain gauge
• Cable needle
• Stitch markers
• Size G/6 (4mm) crochet hook

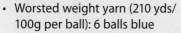

Gauge
22 sts and 26 rows = 4 inches/10cm in pat.

To save time, take time to check gauge.

Special Abbreviations
Make 1 (M1): Insert LH needle from front to back under horizontal strand between last st worked and next st, k1-tbl.

Slip, knit 2 together, pass slipped stitch over (sk2p): Slip next st kwise, k2tog, pass slipped st over st resulting from k2tog to dec 2 sts.

Cable 4 Front (C4F): Slip next 2 sts to cn and hold in front, k2, k2 sts from cn.

Cable 4 Back (C4B): Slip next 2 sts to cn and hold in back, k2, k2 sts from cn.

Special Technique
Crochet Cast-On: Make a slip knot on crochet hook. Holding knitting needle and working yarn in left hand, and crochet hook in right hand, bring working yarn under knitting needle. *With crochet hook, reach over needle and pull a loop through the loop on the crochet hook. Bring yarn back between

needle and crochet hook, under needle, and rep from * until you have 1 less than the desired number of sts. Place loop from crochet hook onto needle.

Pattern Stitch
Eyelets & Wavy-Cables (multiple of 13 sts + 14)
Row 1 (cable side): Sl 1pwise wyif, k4, *k4, p9; rep from * to last 9 sts, k9.
Row 2 (eyelet side): Sl 1pwise wyif, k4, *p4, k1, k2tog, yo, k3, yo, ssk, k1; rep from * to last 9 sts, p4, k5.
Row 3: Sl 1pwise wyif, k4, *C4F, p9; rep from * to last 9 sts, C4F, k5.
Row 4: Sl 1pwise wyif, k4, *p4, k3, yo, sk2p, yo, k3; rep from * to last 9 sts, p4, k5.
Rows 5 and 6: Rep Rows 1 and 2.
Row 7: Sl 1pwise wyif, k4, *C4B, p9; rep from * to last 9 sts, C4B, k5.
Row 8: Rep Row 4.
Rep Rows 1–8 for pat.

Pattern Notes
A circular needle is used to accommodate the large number of stitches; do not join, work back and forth in rows.

Slip the first stitch of each row purlwise, with yarn in front.

The 5-st garter-stitch side borders are worked as blanket is knit.

This blanket is reversible with the cable pattern showing on 1 side and the eyelet pattern visible on the other side.

Blanket
With crochet hook, crochet cast on 167 sts.

Knit 9 rows, slipping first st of each row pwise wyif.

Note: If desired, place markers after first 5 sts and before last 5 sts for garter-st border.

Next row (inc row): Sl 1pwise wyif, k6, [M1, k5, M1, k6] 14 times, M1, k6—196 sts.

Rep Rows 1–8 of Eyelets & Wavy-Cables pat until blanket measures approx 38 inches from beg, ending with Row 8.

Next row (dec row): Sl 1pwise wyif, k5, [k2tog, k7, k2tog, k2] 14 times, k2tog, k6—167 sts.

Knit 9 rows, slipping first st of each row pwise wyif. Bind off loosely.

Block to measurements. ●

Breezy Ruffles Throw

Gentle gathers and lacy stripes are a breeze to knit.

Design by Rena V. Stevens

Skill Level
■■□□ EASY

Finished Sizes
Approx 40 x 45 inches

Materials

- Coats & Clark TLC Essentials (worsted weight; 100% acrylic; 312 yds/170g per skein): 2 skeins each light celery #2615 (A), robin egg #2820 (B), 1 skein butter #2220 (C)
- Size 10½ (6.5mm) circular needle or size needed to obtain gauge

Gauge
14 sts = 4 inches/10cm in St st.

To save time, take time to check gauge.

Special Abbreviation
Increase (inc): Knit into front and back of next st.

Pattern Notes
Circular needle is used to accommodate large number of stitches; do not join, work back and forth in rows.

Slip all stitches purlwise.

Carry yarn loosely across 2 slip stitches on Rows 6–17, except as noted.

Throw
With A, cast on 135 sts.

Rows 1–4: Knit across.

Row 5: Purl across.

Row 6 (RS): *K2, sl 2 wyif; rep from * to last 3 sts, end k3.

Row 7: *P2, sl 2 wyib; rep from * to last 3 sts, end p3.

Row 8: K4, *sl 2 wyif, k2; rep from * to last 3 sts, end sl 2 wyif, k1.

Row 9: P4, *sl 2 wyib, p2; rep from * to last 3 sts, end sl 2 wyib, p1.

Rows 10–17: Rep [Rows 6–9] twice.

Row 18: Knit across.

Rows 19 and 20: With C, purl across.

Row 21: Knit across.

Row 22: *K2, sl 1 wyib; rep from * to last 3 sts, end k3.

Row 23: P3, *sl 1 wyif, p2; rep from * across.

Row 24: K2, *drop sl st off needle in front, k2, pick up and knit dropped st; rep from * to last st, end k1.

Row 25: Purl across.

Row 26: K2, *yo, k2tog, k1; rep from * to last st, end k1.

Row 27: Purl across.

Row 28: K4, *sl 1 wyib, k2; rep from * to last 2 sts, end sl 1 wyib, k1.

Row 29: P1, *sl 1 wyif, p2; rep from * to last 2 sts, end p2.

Row 30: K2, *sl 2 wyib, drop next sl st off needle, put 2 sl sts back on LH needle, pick up and knit dropped st, k2; rep from *, k1.

Row 31: Knit across.

Row 32: Purl across.

Row 33: With B, purl across.

Row 34: Knit across.

Row 35: Purl across.

Rows 36–39: Carrying yarn snugly across sl sts in these 4 rows, rep Rows 6–9.

Row 40: *K1, inc; rep from * across, end k1—202 sts.

Rows 41, 43 and 45: Purl across.

Rows 42 and 44: Knit across.

Row 46: *K1, k2tog; rep from * across, end k1—135 sts.

Row 47: Purl across.

Rows 48–51: Carrying yarn snugly across sl sts in these 4 rows, rep Rows 6–9.

Rows 52–63: Rep Rows 40–51.

Row 64: Knit across.

Rows 65–78: Rep Rows 19–32.

Rows 79–110: With A, rep Rows 33–64.

Rows 111–124: Rep Rows 19–32.

Rows 125–216: Rep Rows 33–124.

Rows 217–219: With B, work in St st.

Rows 220–227: Rep Rows 10–17.

Knit 4 rows, bind off all sts kwise.

Block lightly. ●

Sunny Summer Throw

This throw is the perfect accent for your summer abode. It will add dimension and texture to your decor.

Design by Suzanne Atkinson

. . . .

Skill Level

◼◼◼◼ EXPERIENCED

Finished Size
Approx 42 x 48 inches (blocked)

Materials

- Plymouth Yarn Co. Galway Worsted (worsted weight; 100% wool; 210 yds/100g per ball): 9 balls golden yellow #179
- Size 8 (5mm) 29-inch circular needle or size needed to obtain gauge

Gauge
20 sts and 26 rows = 4 inches/10cm in pat.

To save time, take time to check gauge.

Special Technique
[Yo] 6 times: Wrap yarn around needle 6 times; on next row, k1 in back of each wrap (6 sts inc).

Pattern Notes
Circular needle is used to accommodate large number of stitches; do not join, work back and forth in rows.

Slip first stitch of every row purlwise with yarn in front. Garter stitch edges are worked as afghan is knitted.

Stitch counts vary on each row due to increases and decreases in pattern. Original stitch count is restored on Row 6, so count stitches only after this row.

To bind off in pattern, knit the knit stitches and purl the purl stitches while binding off.

Throw
Cast on 208 sts.

Lower Border
Rows 1 (WS)–6: Sl 1, knit across.

Body
Row 1 (WS): Sl 1, k2, ssp, p3, [yo] 6 times, p3, p2tog, *k1, p2, yo, p2tog, k1, ssp, p3, [yo] 6 times, p3, p2tog; rep from * to last 3 sts, k3—260 sts.

Row 2 (RS): Sl 1, k2, k2tog, k2, [k1-tbl] 6 times, k2, ssk, *p1, k2, yo, ssk, p1, k2tog, k2, [k1-tbl] 6 times, k2, ssk; rep from * to last 3 sts, k3—234 sts.

Row 3: Sl 1, k2, ssp, p1, [yo, p1] 6 times, p1, p2tog,*k1, p2, yo, p2tog, k1, ssp, p1, [yo, p1] 6 times, p1, p2tog; rep from * to last 3 sts, k3—286 sts.

Row 4: Sl 1, k2, k2tog, k12, ssk, *p1, k2, yo, ssk, p1, k2tog, k12, ssk; rep from * to last 3 sts, k3—260 sts.

Row 5: Sl 1, k2, ssp, k10, p2tog, *k1, p2, yo, p2tog, k1, ssp, k10, p2tog; rep from * to last 3 sts, k3—234 sts.

Row 6: Sl 1, k2, k2tog, p8, ssk, *p1, k2, yo, ssk, p1, k2tog, p8, ssk; rep from * to last 3 sts, k3—208 sts.

Rep pat Rows 1–6 until throw measures approx 46 inches from beg, ending with Row 6. (In sample, 44 reps of pat were worked.)

Upper Border
Rows 1 (WS)–6: Sl 1, knit across.

Bind off loosely on WS. ●

Snowballs Afghan

This snowball pattern imitates winter weather, combining warm winter colors and shapes.

Design by Nazanin S. Fard

Skill Level
■■■□ INTERMEDIATE

Finished Size
Approx 48 x 60 inches

Materials
- Red Heart Super Saver (worsted weight; 100% acrylic; solids: 364 yds/7 oz per skein, prints: 244 yds/5 oz per skein): 10 skeins painted desert print #303 (A), 4 skeins aran #313 (B)
- Size 11 (8mm) needles
- Size I/9 (5.5mm) crochet hook
- Tapestry needle

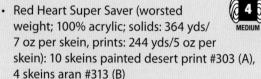

4 MEDIUM

Gauge
12 sts and 16 rows = 4 inches/10cm in St st with 2 strands of yarn held tog.

To save time, take time to check gauge.

Pattern Note
Use 2 strands of yarn held together for entire afghan.

Pattern Stitch
(Multiple of 5 sts + 1)
Row 1 (WS): With A, purl.
Row 2: Knit.
Row 3: *P2, wrap yarn around needle twice, p3, wrap yarn around needle twice, rep from * to last st, end with p1. Do not break yarn.
Row 4: With B, k1, *drop extra wraps, sl 1 wyib, k2, drop extra wraps, sl 1 wyib, (k1, yo, k1, yo, k1) in next st. Rep from * ending with k1.

Row 5: K1, *sl 1 wyif, p2, sl 1 wyif, k5. Rep from * ending with sl 1, p2, sl 1, k1.
Row 6: K1, *sl 1 wyib, k2, sl 1 wyib, p5. Rep from * ending with sl 1, k2, sl 1, k1.
Row 7: K1, *sl 1 wyif, p2, sl 1, wyif, k2tog, k3tog, pass the k2tog st over the k3tog st. Rep from * ending with sl 1, p2, sl 1, k1.
Row 8: With A, k1, *drop first elongated st off needle to front of work, sl 2 wyib, drop next elongated st off needle to front, with LH needle pick up the first elongated st, slip the same 2 sts back to LH needle, then pick up the 2nd elongated st onto LH needle, k5. Rep from * ending with k1.
Rep Rows 1–8 for pat.

Block
Make 20

With A, cast on 31 sts. Knit 5 rows of garter st.

Repeat [Rows 1 - 8 of pat] 5 times.

Knit 5 rows garter st. Bind off loosely.

Finishing

Block
Pick up 31 sts on 1 side of block. Knit 6 rows garter st. Bind off loosely.

Rep for other side.

Afghan
Sew blocks tog in 5 rows of 4 blocks. Block afghan to shape. With B and crochet hook, work 1 row of reverse single crochet around afghan. Fasten off. ●

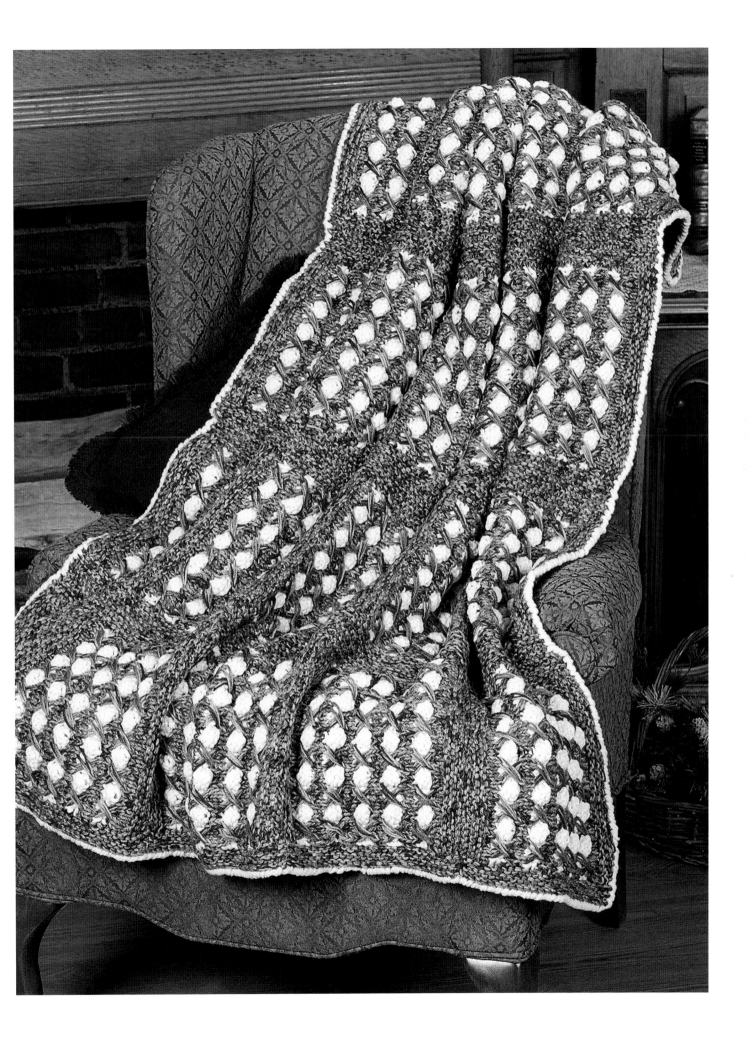

Little Chevron Rib Afghan

This chevron rib afghan looks complicated, but it's a breeze to knit!

Design by Frances Hughes

Skill Level
■■□□ EASY

Finished Size
44 x 62 inches, after blocking

Materials
- Berroco Peruvia Quick (bulky weight; 100% Peruvian Highland wool; 103 yds/ 100g per hank): 9 hanks blanco #9100
- Size 11 (8mm) 32-inch circular needle or size needed to obtain gauge

5 BULKY

Gauge
12 sts and 16 rows = 4 inches/10cm in Chevron Rib pat.

To save time, take time to check gauge.

Pattern Stitch
Chevron Rib
Row 1 (RS): K1, [yo, k2tog] 6 times, p1, *k1, p1, [k2, p1] twice, k1, p1; rep from * to last 13 sts, k1, [yo, k2tog] 6 times.
Row 2: P13, k1, *p2, [k1, p1] twice, k1, p2, k1; rep from * to last 13 sts, p13.

Row 3: K1, [yo, k2tog] 6 times, p1, *k3, p3, k3, p1; rep from * to last 13 sts, k1, [yo, k2tog] 6 times.
Row 4: P13, k2, [p3, k1, p3, k3] 7 times, p3, k1, p3, k2, p13.
Rep Rows 1–4 for pat.

Afghan
Cast on 107 sts.

Border
Row 1: K1, *yo, k2tog; rep from * across.

Row 2: Purl across.

[Rep Rows 1 and 2] 7 times.

Body
[Work Rows 1–4 of Chevron Rib pat] 38 times.

Border
Row 1: K1, *yo, k2tog; rep from * across.

Row 2: Purl across.

[Rep Rows 1 and 2] 7 times, then rep Row 1.

Bind off loosely pwise. Block as desired. ●

Country Living

Imagine cool country breezes gently blowing across your face as you sit

contentedly on the porch, all the while wrapped in warmth as you marvel

at the evening sunset.

Watercolor Prism

Choose soft shades for an afghan that soothes the soul.

Design by Sandy Scoville

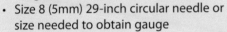

Skill Level
■■□□ EASY

Finished Size
Approx 42 x 60 inches

Materials
- Worsted weight yarn: 6 oz/420 yds/ 180g main color (MC), 4 oz/280 yds/ 120g each of 8 different scrap colors **[4 MEDIUM]**
- Size 8 (5mm) 29-inch circular needle or size needed to obtain gauge
- Size H/8 (5mm) crochet hook (for edging)

Gauge
16 sts = 4 inches/10cm in St st.

To save time, take time to check gauge.

Pattern Notes
Slip all stitches purlwise; carry working color loosely behind slip stitches.

Circular needle used to accommodate stitches; do no join, work back and forth in rows.

Afghan
With MC, cast on 182 sts.

Bottom Border
Row 1 (RS): Knit.

Row 2: Knit.

Body
Row 1: Knit.

Row 2: Purl.

Row 3: With any scrap color, k2, *sl 4, k2; rep from * across.

Row 4: P3, sl 2, *p4, sl 2; rep from * to last 3 sts; p3.

Row 5: Knit.

Row 6: Purl.

Row 7: With new scrap color, k1, sl 2, k2, *sl 4, k2; rep from * to last 3 sts, sl 2, k1.

Row 8: P1, sl 1, p4, *sl 2, p4; rep from * to last 2 sts, sl 1, p1.

Rows 9–32: [Rep Rows 1–8] 3 times more.

Rows 33 and 34: Rep Rows 1 and 2.

Rows 35–38: With MC, rep Rows 3–6.

Rows 39 and 40: With first scrap color used, rep Rows 7 and 8.

Rep Rows 1–8 in established color sequence until afghan measures approx 58 inches, ending with Row 2 or 6.

Row 3 or 7: With MC, work in pat across.

Row 4 or 8: Work in pat across.

Row 5 or 1: Knit.

Row 6 or 2: Purl.

Top Border
Row 1: Knit.

Row 2: Knit.

Bind off all sts.

Edging
Hold afghan with RS facing and 1 short edge at top; with crochet hook and MC, make slip knot on hook and join with a sc in first st.

Rnd 1: Work 2 sc in same sp as joining (beg corner); working across edge, sc in each st to last st; 3 sc in next st (corner); working along next side in ends of rows, work 2 sc for every 3 rows to next short edge; working across next edge, 3 sc in first st (corner); sc in each st to last st; 3 sc in last st (corner); working along next side in ends of rows, work same number of sc as on opposite side; join in joining sc.

Rnd 2: Ch 1, working from left to right, reverse sc in each sc around, working 3 reverse sc in 2nd sc of each corner; join in first reverse sc. Fasten off and weave in all ends. ●

Streaked Stripes

Use all your favorite shades for your own version of this striking afghan.

Design by Sandy Scoville

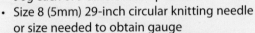

Finished Size
Approx 44 x 60 inches

Materials
- Worsted weight yarn: 18 oz/1,260 yds/ 540g main color (MC), 3 oz/210 yds/ 90g each of 9 different scrap colors
- Size 8 (5mm) 29-inch circular knitting needle or size needed to obtain gauge
- Size H/8 (5mm) crochet hook (for edging)

4 MEDIUM

Gauge
16 sts = 4 inches/10cm in St st.

To save time, take time to check gauge.

Pattern Notes
Slip all stitches purlwise; carry working color loosely behind slip stitches. Carry main color loosely along side edge when not in use.

Afghan
With any scrap color, cast on 185 sts.

Row 1 (RS): Knit.

Row 2: P1, k3, *p3, k3; rep from * to last st, p1.

Row 3: With MC, k4, sl 3, *k3, sl 3; rep from * to last 4 sts, k4.

Row 4: P1, k3, *sl 3, k3; rep from * to last st, p1.

Rows 5–12: With same scrap color, [rep Rows 1–4] twice more.

Row 13: With new scrap color, knit.

Row 14: P4, k3, *p3, k3; rep from * to last 4 sts, p4.

Row 15: With MC, k1, sl 3, *k3, sl 3; rep from * to last st, k1.

Row 16: P1, sl 3; *k3, sl 3; rep from * to last st, p1.

Rows 17–24: With same scrap color, [rep Rows 13–16] twice more.

Rep Rows 1–24 until afghan measures approx 60 inches, ending with a Row 12 or 24.

Next row: With same scrap color, knit.

Bind off all sts.

Side Edging
Hold afghan with RS facing and 1 short edge at top; with crochet hook and MC, make a slip knot on hook and join with a sc in first st, 2 sc in same sp as joining (beg corner); working across edge, sc in each st to last st; 3 sc in next st (corner); working along next side in ends of rows, work 2 sc for every 3 rows to next short edge; working across next edge, 3 sc in first st (corner); sc in each st to last st; 3 sc in next st (corner); working along next side in ends of rows, work same number of sc as on opposite side; join in joining sc. Fasten off and weave in all ends. ●

Dashing Hues

It certainly is dramatic how this afghan changes in feel by just changing the colors!

Design by Sandy Scoville

. . . .

Skill Level

■■■□ INTERMEDIATE

Finished Size
Approx 44 x 60 inches

Materials
- Worsted weight yarn: 26 oz/1,820 yds/ 780g main color (MC), 4 oz/280 yds/ 120g Color A and 2oz/140 yds/ 60g each of 5 different scrap colors
- Size 8 (5mm) circular knitting needle or size needed to obtain gauge
- Tapestry needle

5 BULKY

Gauge
16 sts and 26 rows = 4 inches/10cm in St st (knit 1 row, purl 1 row).

To save time take time to check gauge.

Pattern Notes
Circular needle used to accommodate stitches; do not join, work back and forth in rows.

Carry main color loosely along side edge when not in use.

Slip all stitches purlwise with yarn held to wrong side. When working on wrong side, after slipping stitches, it will be necessary to move yarn under needle to back of work to be in position to knit the following stitches.

Afghan
With MC, cast on 185 sts.

Bottom Border
Rows 1 (RS)–4: Knit.

Body
Rows 1 and 3 (RS): With MC, knit.

Rows 2 and 4: Purl.

Rows 5 and 6: With A, knit.

Rows 7–10: With MC, rep Rows 1–4.

Rows 11 and 12: With any scrap color, k1, sl 3, *k3, sl 1, k3, sl 3; rep from * to last st, k1.

Rows 13 and 14: With MC, rep Rows 1 and 2.

Rows 15 and 16: With same scrap color, rep Rows 11 and 12.

Rows 17 and 18: With MC, rep Rows 1 and 2.

Rows 19 and 20: With same scrap color, rep Rows 11 and 12.

Rep Rows 1–20, changing to new scrap color on Row 11 (using same scrap on reps of Row 11), until afghan measures about 58 inches.

Top Border
With MC, knit 5 rows.

Bind off kwise.

Side Border
With RS facing and using MC, pick up and knit 220 sts evenly spaced along 1 long edge.

Rows 1–4: Knit.

Bind off kwise.

Rep on other long side.

Weave in all ends. ●

Falling Leaves

The brilliant colors of fall come alive in this richly striped afghan.

Design by Sandy Scoville

. . . .

Skill Level
■■■□ INTERMEDIATE

Finished Size
Approx 48 x 64 inches

Materials
- Worsted weight yarn: 18 oz/1,260 yds/ 540g main color (MC), 4 oz/280 yds/ 120g of 8 different scrap colors
- Size 10 (6mm) 29-inch circular knitting needle

Gauge
16 sts = 4 inches/10cm in St st.

To save time, take time to check gauge.

Pattern Notes
Slip all stitches purlwise.

Circular needle used to accommodate stitches; do not join, work back and forth in rows.

Afghan
With MC, cast on 181 sts.

Bottom Border
Row 1 (RS): Knit.

Rows 2 and 3: Rep Row 1.

Body
Row 1 (WS): K4, purl to last 4 sts, k4.

Row 2 (RS): Knit.

Note: On following row, when working yo's, wrap yarn completely around the needle and back to front twice.

Row 3: K4, p3, yo twice, *p4, yo twice; rep from * to last 6 sts, end p2, k4.

Row 4: With any scrap color, k6; drop yo's, sl 1; *k1, insert RH needle in next st on 2nd row below st on needle, draw up loop, knit st on needle, pass loop over; k1, drop yo's, sl 1; rep from * to last 6 sts, k6.

Row 5: K4, p2, sl 1, *p3, sl 1; rep from * to last 6 sts, p2, k4.

Row 6: Knit.

Row 7: K4, p3; yo twice, *p4, yo twice; rep from * to last 6 sts, p2, k4.

Rows 8–35: [Rep Rows 4–7] 7 times more, changing to new scrap color on each Row 4.

Row 36: With MC, rep Row 4.

Row 37: Rep Row 5.

Row 38: Knit.

Row 39: K4, purl to last 4 sts, k4.

Rows 40–53: [Rep Rows 38 and 39] 7 times more.

Row 54: Knit.

Row 55: Rep Row 3.

[Rep Rows 4–55] 4 times more.

[Rep Rows 4–39] once.

Top Border
Row 1: With MC, knit.

Rows 2 and 3: Rep Row 1.

Bind off. ●

Harmonious Stripes

Stripes of many colors are created with a main color and fourteen colors of scrap yarn—a great use for your stash!

Design by Sandy Scoville

. . . .

Skill Level
 EASY

Finished Size
Aprox 40 x 60 inches

Materials
- Worsted weight yarn: 10 oz/700 yds/ 300g main color (MC), 3½ oz/245 yds/ 105g each of 14 scrap colors
- Size 8 (5mm) 29-inch circular knitting needle

Gauge
16 sts = 4 inches/10 cm in St st.

To save time, take time to check gauge.

Pattern Note
Circular needle used to accommodate stitches; do not join, work back and forth in rows.

Afghan
With any scrap, cast on 181 sts.

Bottom Border
Row 1 (RS): Knit.

Rows 2–4: Rep Row 1.

Body
Row 1 (RS): K1, *k5, p1; rep from * to last 6 sts, k6.

Row 2: K1, *p5, k1; rep from * across.

Rows 3–6: [Rep Rows 1 and 2] twice.

Row 7: With MC, knit.

Row 8: K1, *k5, p1; rep from * to last 6 sts, k6.

Row 9: K1; *p5, k1; rep from * across.

Rows 10 and 11: Rep Rows 8 and 9.

Row 12: Rep Row 8.

Row 13: With any scrap, knit.

Row 14: K1, *p5, k1; rep from * across.

Row 15: K1, *k5, p1; rep from * to last 6 sts, k6.

Rows 16 and 17: Rep Rows 14 and 15.

Row 18: Rep Row 14.

Row 19: K1, *p5, k1; rep from * across.

Row 20: K1, *k5, p1; rep from * to last 6 sts, k6.

Rows 21–24: [Rep Rows 19 and 20] twice.

Rows 25–30: With same scrap, rep Rows 13–18.

[Rep Rows 7–30] 12 times more.

[Rep Rows 7–12] once.

With same scrap color as Row 1, rep Rows 13–18.

Top Border
Row 1: With same scrap color, knit.

Rows 2 and 3: Rep Row 1.

Bind off. ●

General Information

Standard Abbreviations

[ ] work instructions within brackets as many times as directed

( ) work instructions within parentheses in the place directed

** repeat instructions following the asterisks as directed

* repeat instructions following the single asterisk as directed

" inch(es)

approx approximately
beg begin/begins/beginning
CC contrasting color
ch chain stitch
cm centimeter(s)
cn cable needle
dec decrease/decreases/decreasing
dpn(s) double-point needle(s)
g gram(s)
inc increase/increases/increasing
k knit

k2tog knit 2 stitches together
kwise knitwise
LH left hand
m meter(s)
M1 make one stitch
MC main color
mm millimeter(s)
oz ounce(s)
p purl
pat(s) pattern(s)
p2tog purl 2 stitches together
psso pass slipped stitch over
pwise purlwise
rem remain/remains/remaining
rep repeat(s)
rev St st reverse stockinette stitch
RH right hand
rnd(s) rounds
RS right side
skp slip, knit, pass slipped stitch over—1 stitch decreased

sk2p slip 1, knit 2 together, pass slipped stitch over the knit 2 together—2 stitches decreased
sl slip
sl 1kwise slip 1 knitwise
sl 1pwise slip 1 purlwise
sl st slip stitch(es)
ssk slip, slip, knit these 2 stitches together—a decrease
st(s) stitch(es)
St st stockinette stitch
tbl through back loop(s)
tog together
WS wrong side
wyib with yarn in back
wyif with yarn in front
yd(s) yard(s)
yfwd yarn forward
yo (yo's) yarn over(s)

Standard Yarn Weight System

Categories of yarn, gauge ranges, and recommended needle sizes

Yarn Weight Symbol & Category Names	1 SUPER FINE	2 FINE	3 LIGHT	4 MEDIUM	5 BULKY	6 SUPER BULKY
Type of Yarns in Category	Sock, Fingering, Baby	Sport, Baby	DK, Light Worsted	Worsted, Afghan, Aran	Chunky, Craft, Rug	Bulky, Roving
Knit Gauge Range* in Stockinette Stitch to 4 inches	27–32 sts	23–26 sts	21–24 sts	16–20 sts	12–15 sts	6–11 sts
Recommended Needle in Metric Size Range	2.25–3.25mm	3.25–3.75mm	3.75–4.5mm	4.5–5.5mm	5.5–8mm	8mm and larger
Recommended Needle U.S. Size Range	1 to 3	3 to 5	5 to 7	7 to 9	9 to 11	11 and larger

* GUIDELINES ONLY: The above reflect the most commonly used gauges and needle sizes for specific yarn categories.

Knitting Needle Conversion Chart

U.S.	1	2	3	4	5	6	7	8	9	10	10½	11	13	15	17	19	35	50
Continental-mm	2.25	2.75	3.25	3.5	3.75	4	4.5	5	5.5	6	6.5	8	9	10	12.75	15	19	25

Inches Into Millimeters & Centimeters
All measurements are rounded off slightly.

inches	mm	cm	inches	cm	inches	cm	inches	cm
⅛	3	0.3	5	12.5	21	53.5	38	96.5
¼	6	0.6	5½	14	22	56.0	39	99.0
⅜	10	1.0	6	15.0	23	58.5	40	101.5
½	13	1.3	7	18.0	24	61.0	41	104.0
⅝	15	1.5	8	20.5	25	63.5	42	106.5
¾	20	2.0	9	23.0	26	66.0	43	109.0
⅞	22	2.2	10	25.5	27	68.5	44	112.0
1	25	2.5	11	28.0	28	71.0	45	114.5
1¼	32	3.2	12	30.5	29	73.5	46	117.0
1½	38	3.8	13	33.0	30	76.0	47	119.5
1¾	45	4.5	14	35.5	31	79.0	48	122.0
2	50	5.0	15	38.0	32	81.5	49	124.5
2½	65	6.5	16	40.5	33	84.0	50	127.0
3	75	7.5	17	43.0	34	86.5		
3½	90	9.0	18	46.0	35	89.0		
4	100	10.0	19	48.5	36	91.5		
4½	115	11.5	20	51.0	37	94.0		

Skill Levels

BEGINNER

Beginner projects
for first-time knitters
using basic stitches.
Minimal shaping.

EASY

Easy projects using
basic stitches, repetitive
stitch patterns, simple
color changes and
simple shaping
and finishing.

INTERMEDIATE

Intermediate projects
with a variety of stitches,
mid-level shaping
and finishing.

EXPERIENCED

Experienced projects
using advanced tech-
niques and stitches,
detailed shaping and
refined finishing.

Knitting Basics

Cast-On

Leaving an end about an inch long for each stitch to be cast on, make a slip knot on the right needle.

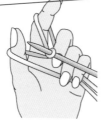

Place the thumb and index finger of your left hand between the yarn ends with the long yarn end over your thumb, and the strand from the skein over your index finger. Close your other fingers over the strands to hold them against your palm. Spread your thumb and index fingers apart and draw the yarn into a "V."

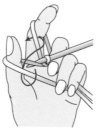

Place the needle in front of the strand around your thumb and bring it underneath this strand. Carry the needle over and under the strand on your index finger.

Draw through loop on thumb.

Drop the loop from your thumb and draw up the strand to form a stitch on the needle.

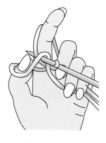

Repeat until you have cast on the number of stitches indicated in the pattern. Remember to count the beginning slip knot as a stitch.

Cable Cast-On

This type of cast-on is used when adding stitches in the middle or at the end of a row.

Make a slip knot on the left needle. Knit a stitch in this knot and place it on the left needle. Insert the right needle between the last two stitches on the left needle. Knit a stitch and place it on the left needle. Repeat for each stitch needed.

Knit (k)

Insert tip of right needle from front to back in next stitch on left needle.

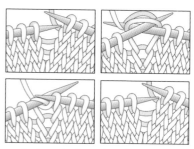

Bring yarn under and over the tip of the right needle.

Pull yarn loop through the stitch with right needle point.

Slide the stitch off the left needle. The new stitch is on the right needle.

Purl (p)

With yarn in front, insert tip of right needle from back to front through next stitch on the left needle.

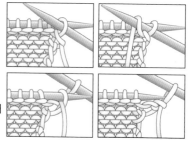

Bring yarn around the right needle counterclockwise.

With right needle, draw yarn back through the stitch.

Slide the stitch off the left needle. The new stitch is on the right needle.

Bind-Off

Binding off (knit)

Knit first two stitches on left needle. Insert tip of left needle into first stitch worked on right needle and pull it over the second stitch and completely off the needle.

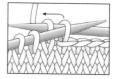

Knit the next stitch and repeat. When one stitch remains on right needle, cut yarn and draw tail through last stitch to fasten off.

Binding off (purl)

Purl first two stitches on left needle. Insert tip of left needle into first stitch worked on right needle and pull it over the second stitch and completely off the needle.

Purl the next stitch and repeat. When one stitch remains on right needle, cut yarn and draw tail through last stitch to fasten off.

Increase (inc)

Two stitches in one stitch

Increase (knit)
Knit the next stitch in the usual manner, but don't remove the stitch from the left needle. Place right needle behind left needle and knit again into the back of the same stitch. Slip original stitch off left needle.

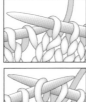

Increase (purl)
Purl the next stitch in the usual manner, but don't remove the stitch from the left needle. Place right needle behind left needle and purl again into the back of the same stitch. Slip original stitch off left needle.

Invisible Increase (M1)
There are several ways to make or increase one stitch.

Make 1 with Left Twist (M1L)
Insert left needle from front to back under the horizontal loop between the last stitch worked and next stitch on left needle.

With right needle, knit into the back of this loop.

To make this increase on the purl side, insert left needle in same manner and purl into the back of the loop.

Make 1 with Right Twist (M1R)
Insert left needle from back to front under the horizontal loop between the last stitch worked and next stitch on left needle.

With right needle, knit into the front of this loop.

To make this increase on the purl side, insert left needle in same manner and purl into the front of the loop.

Make 1 with Backward Loop over the right needle
With your thumb, make a loop over the right needle.

Slip the loop from your thumb onto the needle and pull to tighten.

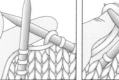

Make 1 in top of stitch below
Insert tip of right needle into the stitch on left needle one row below.

Knit this stitch, then knit the stitch on the left needle.

Decrease (dec)

Knit 2 together (k2tog)
Put tip of right needle through next two stitches on left needle as to knit. Knit these two stitches as one.

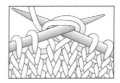

Purl 2 together (p2tog)
Put tip of right needle through next two stitches on left needle as to purl. Purl these two stitches as one.

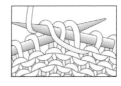

Slip, Slip, Knit (ssk)
Slip next two stitches, one at a time, as to knit from left needle to right needle.

Insert left needle in front of both stitches and work off needle together.

Slip, Slip, Purl (ssp)
Slip next two stitches, one at a time, as to knit from left needle to right needle. Slip these stitches back onto left needle keeping them twisted. Purl these two stitches together through back loops.

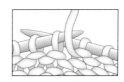

Fringe Instructions

Basic Instructions

Cut a piece of cardboard half as long as specified in instructions for strands plus ½ inch for trimming allowance. Wind yarn loosely and evenly lengthwise around cardboard. When card is filled, cut yarn across one end. Do this several times, and then begin fringing; you can wind additional strands as you need them.

Single-Knot Fringe

Hold specified number of strands for one knot of fringe together, and then fold in half. Hold afghan with right side facing you. Use crochet hook to draw folded end through space or stitch from right to wrong side (Figures 1 and 2), pull loose ends through folded section (Figure 3) and draw knot up firmly (Figure 4). Space knots as indicated in pattern instructions.

Double-Knot Fringe

Begin by working single-knot fringe completely across one end of afghan. With right side facing, and working from left to right, take half the strands of one knot and half the strands in the knot next to it, and knot them together (Figure 5).

Figure 1

Figure 2

Figure 3

Figure 4

Single-Knot Fringe

Double-Knot Fringe

Figure 5

Photo Index

....

7

11

13

17

19

23

27

28

29

30

33

35

37

39

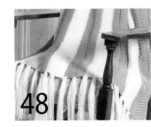

40

43

47

48

50

53

54

57

59

60

63

65

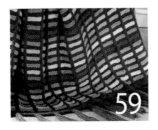

67

68

71

73

76

77

79

80

83

86

88

90

92

94

97

101

102

104

107

108

110

113

115

117

119

120